A Time of Change

A History of the Southland Presbytery of the Presbyterian Church of Aotearoa New Zealand 1990 to 2010

Rev Heather Kennedy

Philip
Garside
Publishing Ltd.

Contact Heather at
email: rev.heather.kennedy@gmail.com

We gratefully acknowledge the funding support for this
book provided by The Southland Heritage Trust and the
Southern Presbytery of the Presbyterian Church of Aotearoa
New Zealand

Paperback International edition 2023:
ISBN 9781991027504

Also available

New Zealand Paperback: ISBN 9781991027498
Paperback print-on-demand USA: ISBN 9798398872873
PDF: ISBN 9781991027511
ePub: ISBN 9781991027528

Philip Garside Publishing Ltd
PO Box 17160
Wellington 6147
New Zealand

books@pgpl.co.nz — www.philipgarsidebooks.com

Cover design based on:
Southland, regional council of New Zealand, on white. Relief
ID 194975268 © Yarr65 | Dreamstime.com

Contents

Contents

Preface

In order to look at the parishes and events in the Southland Presbytery in the last twenty years of its existence, the following is a brief history of parishes who made up the presbytery in 2010.

Much of this material has been researched from the following historic publications:

- James Chisholm's *Fifty Years Syne*, published in Dunedin, NZ by the New Zealand Bible Tract and Book Society in 1898.
- John Collie's *The Story of the Otago Free Church Settlement 1848-1948*, published in Dunedin, NZ by the Presbyterian Bookroom in 1948.
- Georgina McDonald's *The Flame Unquenched: Being the History of the Presbyterian Church in Southland in the Years 1856-1956,* published in Invercargill, NZ by the Presbytery of Southland in 1956, and
- Rev Crawford Madill's *Part of a Miracle: Profile of a Presbytery – Southland 1956-1990,* published in Invercargill, NZ by the Presbytery of Southland in 1990.

In completing the record of parish details, much of the information has been obtained from Southland Presbytery minutes, mostly stored at the Church Archive Centre in Dunedin and parish annual reports. Some members of parishes have also been helpful in providing information from their own memories and experiences. My apologies for any errors and omissions.

Chapter 1 – 150 years:
Parishes of Southland Presbytery 1860–2010

The Settlement of the Free Church of Scotland (Presbyterians) in Southland

When the surveyor Mr Tuckett anchored in the ship *'Deborah'* at New River Heads on 18 May 1844, he was not impressed with the prospects of settlement in the region, describing it as a 'land of ceaseless rain, dripping bush, boundless swamps and deep creeks.' There were European settlers at Jacob's River living peacefully alongside Māori under the 'beneficent sway' of Captain John Howell, who had probably arrived in 1837. The New Zealand Company was dissolved in 1850, so southern land was bought from Māori by the government in 1853, with payment of £2,600 being paid on 15 February 1854. At this time, the site at the head of the New River estuary was named Invercargill, and what is now Bluff was named Campbelltown. Surveyors supervised by Mr John Turnbull Thompson arrived, and during October 1856 'the town of Invercargill was laid off and 2½ million acres of the surrounding country was triangulated.'

Captain Elles was stationed at Campbelltown (Bluff) as the Collector of Customs and then moved to Invercargill on 1 February 1858, to be appointed the Receiver of Land Revenue. At the time, Invercargill was mostly covered in bush; there were about 12 houses, two hotels and two stores in Tay Street. It was difficult to reach Invercargill overland due to swamps and creeks, so most supplies arrived by sea from Dunedin, over the bar into the New River to a berth on the Puni Creek, a journey of three to six weeks, depending on the weather. In 1855, the land between the Mataura River and the Oreti River remained uninhabited and undeveloped. By 1858, the growing town of Invercargill had added two banks, two shops, a carpentry, a saddler, a cobbler, a smithy, a bakery, a butchery, a cricket ground, a prison, barracks and private residences. In December 1858, there was near famine when the 40 residents had to go without supplies because ships sheltered at Waikawa on the trip from Dunedin due to 'contrary winds,' and many inventive means were employed to compensate for the non-arrival of provisions.

Those wishing to get married at this time had to call on either Rev Bannerman, who travelled on foot from his home at Waipahi or cross to Ruapuke Island (in an open boat) for Rev Johann Friedrick Heinrich Wohlers (Bavarian pastor) to solemnise the union. Tales were told of the sad fate of an entire wedding party of six, all of whom perished by drowning on the 7 December 1858, when the boat they were travelling in hit the sandbank when crossing the New River bar and capsized while they were on their way to the island for the wedding.

The population of Murihiku (Southland) was growing slowly, and settlers, due to their isolation from Dunedin, 'became seized with a strong desire to manage their own affairs.' Therefore, Southland was proclaimed a separate province from 1 April 1861, with a Provincial Council made up of 11 councillors, representing six electoral districts, for a total of 269 electors, with Captain Elles appointed the Commissioner and Treasurer. The first edition of *The Southland News* was published on 16 February 1861, and the first coach journey from Invercargill to Dunedin was made on 6 April 1864. Trains from Invercargill to Bluff started in February 1867, with trains going through to Dunedin from 22 January 1879. Further parishes in rural Southland were then established as land was surveyed and sold for farming. These parishes met the needs of those settling in the area, with membership made up of landowners, staff, workers and those who lived in the near vicinity, especially as commerce and trade was developing and towns started to emerge.

Over the intervening 150 years or so, the location and make-up of parishes in Southland has changed due to various influences. The following is a look at the history of the parishes of the Southland Presbytery as at 2010 in the order in which they were founded, the establishment of the parish, the merger with other parishes in the region and the minsters that served in the parish over the years since they began.

Riverton – 40kms west of Invercargill city centre

In 1835 a fleet of ships under the command of Captain John Howell made the headquarters for their activities of catching whales, muttonbirds, crayfish and oysters, in the estuary of the Aparima River at Riverton, formerly known as Jacob's River. They cleared the bush and undergrowth and made camp on the south side of the river and Captain Howell made friends with the Ngāti Māmoe Māori on the other side of the river, with the not unexpected influx of half-caste children. Captain Howell also married a Māori princess, gaining a large acreage of land between Aparima and Waimatuku, settling in Riverton. As early as 1844, children we taught scripture and gathered for worship. Bishop Selwyn in his travels around New Zealand held a worship service in Riverton in 1844, followed by visits from Wesleyan preachers.

The Second charge in the Southland region was the ministry of Rev Lachlan McGilvray in April 1861, in Riverton followed shortly thereafter by Rev James Clark in April 1864.

The Presbyterian parish at Orepuki worked closely with Home Missions at Colac Bay, Pahia and Round Hill. These were gold-mining areas with significant numbers of Chinese miners. A Chinese Christian Evangelist, Paul Ah Chin was asked to work with these miners alongside Mr H. Cowie who had been a missionary in China, but neither spoke Cantonese. Rev Alexander Don was sent to China to learn Cantonese and on his return served at Round Hill. He resided in Riverton until 1886 and was followed by Chinese catechist Kwok Wai Shang who left to join Rev Don in Lawrence as many of the Chinese miners had moved there.

Orepuki parish joined with Tuatapere in 1941, and Round Hill and Pahia joined Colac Bay, which later joined Riverton parish in 1923. Ministers who had served in Colac Bay, were not ordained to the charge, but provided supply from 1900 to 1923 for one to three years. Three preaching stations were maintained by Riverton parish until 1973 when the parish united with the Methodist congregation to form the Riverton Union Parish. In 1898 the parish recorded a membership of 145, with six Elders and seven Deacons. In 1956, 12 Elders and 5 Deacons were recorded.

Ministers who undertook the charge of Riverton parish after Rev J. Clark were:

- 1872 Rev C.S. Ross
- 1878 Rev J. Cameron
- 1887 Rev T. Neave
- 1898 Rev R. McCully
- 1904 Rev C.A. Gray
- 1923 Rev J. Fordyce
- 1931 Rev A McFarlane
- 1940 Rev J.A.F. Watson
- 1945 Rev L. Jones
- 1949 Rev H.S. Manson
- 1960 Rev R.A. Simpson
- 1967 Rev J.H. Clark

Then as a Union parish:

- 1973 Rev W.H. Blundell (Methodist)
- 1981 Rev Neil Cowie
- 1988 Rev M. Emslie (Methodist)
- 2002 Rev Doris Elphick (Methodist)
- 2007 Local Ministry Team

Oban, Halfmoon Bay, Stewart Island – 40 kms south by sea from Bluff

Stewart Island was, from as early as 1802, a centre for sealers, and later there was a considerable Norwegian presence – whaling, sealing and logging. The Anglican Bishop Selwyn visited and performed marriages and baptisms in 1844. Mr John Murdoch requested a Minister to serve the settlers, and as he was an Elder at First Church who owned a sawmill on the island, he was commissioned to provide for the spiritual welfare of the islanders. Mrs Charles Traill, who resided on Ulva Island in Paterson Inlet, provided Sunday school lessons for children at The Neck, Bravo Island and Halfmoon Bay (Oban). Rev Stobo visited Stewart Island in 1874, conducting worship services at The Neck, Halfmoon Bay and Fort William. He later installed Mr Arthur Traill as a missionary stationed at The Neck.

Rev Wohlers, the non-denominational North German Mission Society missionary arrived on Ruapuke Island in 1844, after a short stay in Motueka, to minister to the Māori on the island. He later transferred to Stewart Island to minister to the resident Presbyterians after the decline of the population on Ruapuke. His daughter Gretchen married Mr Arthur Traill in 1878 and settled at The Neck on Stewart Island, where Brother Wohlers died in 1885. In 1884, an inter-denominational building was built for the Union Church at Halfmoon Bay, administered by trustees from the Presbyterian, Congregational, Salvation Army and Brethren denominations, with Mr Traill as the Presbyterian representative. The Union church arrangement however was not successful, especially in the provision of ministers, and the Presbyterians proceeded to purchase land and build a church and manse on a bush-clad promontory overlooking Halfmoon Bay. The church was opened in 1904, and centenary celebrations were held there ten years ago. The manse was replaced in 1930, and a Sunday School Hall, which was relocated from the Norwegian whaling base, has recently been sold and converted into a private home.

Stewart Island Presbyterian Church has been served over the years of its existence by a variety of Ordained Ministers, Stated Supply and Home Missioners, many for very short periods of time. Sometimes the Minister at Bluff visited on a regular basis, but more recently under the oversight of an Interim Moderator, the parish has welcomed those who have travelled to the island to conduct worship as part of a short stay of a few days, or a few weeks, or sometimes a few months. The parish joined the Regional Resource Ministry in order to provide support for their leaders and resources for the parish as well as oversight and a point of connection with the wider church. The parish currently has four Elders who manage the day-to-day administration and the hospitality of visiting ministers and preachers, with oversight from Rev Heather Kennedy as Interim Moderator.

First Church – Invercargill city centre

One of the earliest settlers in Southland was Rev Alexander Bethune, who arrived from Green Island on 6 November 1856 and conducted the first service of worship in Murihiku, at Kelly's Point (now the corner of Tay and Clyde Streets). He built a house on farmland at Myross Bush, opened a private school in Invercargill and ministered to the settlers there, leading worship each Sunday either in a hotel, the prison, a store or eventually in the courthouse. The Otago Presbytery placed Invercargill under the oversight of Rev Dr William Bannerman, who travelled overland whenever he was able to visit, occasionally being relieved by Rev William Will or Rev Thomas

Burns. These visits encouraged the worshippers, who sought to have their own minister at the 'earliest possible date.' This was conveyed by Rev Bannerman to the Otago Presbytery in mid-1859, and it was agreed in August that year to send for a minister from 'home' (Scotland). A congregation was organised (by Rev Will and Rev Burns) that consisted of 105 members who received Holy Communion for the first time in January 1860. Rev Andrew Stobo from Scotland duly arrived to take up the new charge in Invercargill on 18 May 1860, being ordained and inducted on 29 June by Rev Bannerman and Todd at a service held in the Courthouse. The first meeting of session was held on 14 November 1860, with Rev Bethune appointed Session Clerk. Captain Elles became a Deacon and the Treasurer.

From the outset Rev Stobo was ready to carry the Gospel to distant settlements, such as Bluff and Riverton and visited the goldfields in Central Otago, which were a four days' journey each way. He also regularly took services at Woodlands (Long Bush). A minister was requested there, and Rev Thomas Alexander arrived in 1864. A new schoolhouse was erected in Tay Street shortly after Rev Stobo's arrival in Invercargill, and the congregation moved there for worship services until the original First Church building was opened on 15 March 1863. Invercargill prospered as a result of the gold rush in 1862, though this lasted for only a few years. When a second minister, Rev Andrew Stevens, arrived from Scotland to form a second congregation in July 1865 there was little support for the plan, so he was sent to work with settlers at Wallacetown. Other settlements also requested ministers, especially Riverton, with the result that Rev Lachlan McGilvray arrived, and was followed shortly thereafter by Rev James Clark.

In the 1870s it was identified that a second charge was necessary in Invercargill so steps were undertaken to establish a Second Presbyterian Church in Invercargill. This was brought about through the movement of many members from First Church joining this new parish, which diminished their status as one of the largest Presbyterian parishes in New Zealand, leaving them with only 575 members, which was nonetheless almost six times their number when first established. In 1898 the parish had 532 members, with 14 Elders and 28 Deacons. In 1956 there were 25 Elders and 33 Deacons.

In 2004, the Parish agreed to merge the Kirk Session and Deacon's Courts to form a Parish Council with six Committees. The Committees oversaw Finance, Property and Works, Christian Education, Pastoral matters including visiting District Elders and assistants, Worship and Community Outreach, with two Elders from each committee being members of the Parish Council. Deacons were conferred the office of Elder or Deacon Emeritus. In 2010 the parish had 20 Elders, five Elders Emeriti, four Deacons Emeriti and two Parish Councillors.

Ministers who were ordained to the charge at First Church following on from the pioneering work of Rev A. Bethune were as follows:

- 1860 Rev A Stobo
- 1880 Rev J. Ferguson
- 1894 Rev J.G. Smith
- 1903 Rev R. Ferguson
- 1909 Rev R.M. Ryburn
- 1919 Rev J.L. Robinson
- 1931 Rev A.G.M. Carter
- 1937 Rev J.A. Thomson, who died suddenly while on tour of the country as Assembly Moderator.
- 1945 Rev A. McG. Kirkwood (associate)
- 1949 Rev C.A. Ritchie (Associate)
- 1952 Rev W.J. Pellow
- 1959 Rev Ian Cairns (Stated Supply)
- 1960 Rev Sefton Campbell
- 1967 Rev Crawford Madill
- 1981 Rev Dr Ian Cairns
- 1984 Rev Dr Robert (Bob) J. Eyles
- 1991 Rev Brian J. Williscroft
- 2001 Rev Dr Simon H. Rae
- 2006 Rev Richard J. Gray, then in 2008 with Rev Heather Kennedy (Assistant)

The Parish celebrated in November 2010 the 150th year of the parish with a weekend of events and worship services. The parish had at that time a roll of 266 members with an average attendance at Sunday morning worship of 110.

Bluff / Greenhills – 28 kms south of Invercargill city centre

In the late 1850s, both Rev William Will and Rev Dr William Bannerman made journeys on foot south of their charge in the Taieri to Invercargill. Rev Bannerman even made it to the Bluff, visiting the early settlers in the area and returning from time to time to nurture these members of his flock. The Bluff had also been visited by Bishop Selwyn on his journey around New Zealand in 1844. Rev Bethune presided at the first Presbyterian service of worship in Bluff in 1867 to a very small gathering, as Bluff was a very small port town compared to the port at Riverton. Rev Arnot was employed to consider the possibility of a home mission charge which would include Bluff (known as Campbelltown), but due to difficulties in setting this up, the Presbyterians in Bluff worshipped with the Primitive Methodists and were included in the charge of First Church session. A Mr Green took charge of a home mission including Clifton, Woodend and Bluff, followed by Rev A. Stobo, and then Rev William Hain (formerly a First Church parishioner).

Bluff was later separated from Clifton and Woodend when St. Andrew's (South Invercargill) Parish was established. The town of Bluff had grown somewhat and the port was then able to accommodate large ocean-going vessels, so the task of buying land and plans for a church and manse were commenced.

The parish was established at Bluff in 1894 under the charge of Rev J. Anderson Gardiner, with 4 elders, ten deacons and 52 members. It was possibly the most southern parish in the world, including preaching places at Ocean Beach and Greenhills. Rev Gardiner was soon called to a post in Sydney, Australia, and was replaced by Rev Walter MacLaren. His successor, Rev Alfred Laishley, 1903, became well known as the father of daughters who instigated the Busy Bees Hives, which focused on Biblical teaching, entertainment and support for missionaries overseas, which spread throughout Presbyterian churches in New Zealand. (I attended a 'hive' in Feilding in my youth.) Ministers that followed were:

- 1913 Rev Edward Walker
- 1919 Rev Robert Francis
- 1927 Rev Samuel Waddell
- 1932 Rev Thomas Speer
- 1939 Rev Arthur Ferguson
- 1943 Rev David Hay
- 1944 Rev Frederick Robertson
- 1946 Rev George Jeffreys
- 1952 Rev Barry Doig

Rev Doig also oversaw the home mission at Stewart Island, as there have been strong links between Bluff and 'The Island' over the years.

In 1956 the parish had five elders and eight deacons. Rev Leslie Gibb arrived in 1961, Rev Alfred Willoughby in 1965, Rev Eric Uden in 1970 during whose time, in 1979, the parish became part of the Bluff-Greenhills Co-operating Parish, amalgamating with the Methodist and Anglican congregations and meeting thereafter in the Methodist building.

As a co-operating venture, the parish rotated the oversight from the partner churches, with part-time ministers who no longer resided in Bluff but who were in charges in Invercargill. This system of ministry supply commenced with:

- 1982 Rev Robert (Bob) Short (Methodist)
- 1985 Rev Howard Smith (Presbyterian)
- 1990 Rev Alec Clark (Anglican)
- 1995 Rev Colin Leadley (Methodist)
- 2000 Rev Guus Lukkein (Anglican)
- 2005 Heather Kennedy (Presbyterian), later Rev Heather Kennedy (2008)

Heather Kennedy was seconded from First Presbyterian Church in Invercargill to provide ministry supply quarter-time, until the parish joined the Southland Regional Resource Ministry. The role of Minister in Bluff also included the responsibility of Port Chaplain from 1963, along with membership of the Seafarer's Welfare Centre and the committee that administered it. This role has been taken on by the parish as a whole. The congregation of approximately 30 members has no Methodists, some nominal Presbyterians, and five Anglican members with others who have joined more recently from a variety of faith traditions.

Wallacetown – 15 kms north-west of Invercargill

The first service of worship was conducted by Rev Dr Thomas Burns (on his travels) in 1858. Rev William Will had accompanied him on his visit to Invercargill, as he had recently retired from serving in the Taieri and Clutha and was then appointed to oversee the Wallacetown congregation until the appointment of Rev Stevens in 1866. Rev Stevens had come from the Free Church in Scotland and was noted for covering large distances in the parish – which included

Winton Bush and Centre Bush – on his horse. He was also noted for teaching children the Catechism, which may have been why they hid in the bush when they heard his horse approaching.

The parish grew to include Forest Hill until the Winton Parish and Forest Hill Parish were formed, along with Dipton, Browns, Oreti Plains and Drummond Parishes. Then Waikiwi (which was slowly being settled) was added to Wallacetown and later Waianawa and Ryal Bush. In 1881, Rev James Hutton MacKenzie was called to the parish from Scotland, and he served until 1891, during which time he was also Clerk of Assembly and was the 'guiding spirit' of the writing of the Book of Order. Ministers that followed were:

- 1891 Rev William White
- 1904 Rev James Burrows
- 1911 Rev Adam Begg
- 1918 Rev James Ponder
- 1921 Rev Walter French
- 1926 Rev Duncan McKenzie
- 1933 Rev Leonard Whitehead
- 1939 Rev James Olliver
- 1946 Rev Laurence Ker
- 1964 Rev Thomas Lewis
- 1968 Rev Ross Thompson
- 1975 Rev John Scarlet
- 1984 Rev James (Jim) Young (formerly a member of the parish, now serving in Malawi with his wife who is a Medical Practitioner)
- 1998 Rev Geoff Holding

Since 2003 the parish has been served by members of the Session with a Moderating Elder. In 1903, a branch of the PWMU (Presbyterian Women's Missionary Union) was formed which, as APW (Association of Presbyterian Women), closed in 2003. For a short while in 2005 a Lay Supply Worker, Mr Don McLeod, was employed to serve in the community. A Youth Worker was also employed for a short while. Church membership in 1898 was recorded as five Elders, six Deacons and 172 members; in 1956 there were five Elders and 17 Deacons. The parish had four Elders and six Deacons, with four Elders and two Deacons on Session in 2010, who serve as Ministry Team for a congregation of 30 members. The properties at Waianawa and Ryal Bush have been sold off. Wallacetown is no longer a rural centre and is mostly a satellite settlement of Invercargill.

Woodlands (Longbush) – 20kms east of Invercargill centre.

In 1860 Rev A. Stobo after leading worship at First Church would then walk (nine miles) 16 kilometres to Long Bush to conduct a service there as well. Land in the area was being developed for farming and in 1863 Mr Matthew Holmes offered some of his land for the building of a church and manse, gifting £100 towards the building costs and £100 for a minister's stipend. Rev Thomas Alexander agreed to come from Edinburgh to minister in Longbush and Oteramika. After a period of Supply at Riverton he was inducted at Woodlands in July 1864. He also covered the Winton area, which extended to the Mataura River and the Hokonui Hills. A small church was built between Oteramika and One Tree Point in 1866 and another at Mabel Bush in 1867, when a manse was built at Long Bush for the recently married Rev Alexander. After the railway to Invercargill was completed, it was decided the best site for the church to be erected would be at Woodlands. It was built in 1873 along with a manse. Rev Alexander served for 23 years. As churches were established in the area of his pastoral charge his oversight was focussed on the Woodlands area, being Long Bush, Oteramika, Mabel Bush and Woodlands. In 1891, the parish was deemed too large so further charges were established at Rimu, Kapuka and Oteramika to serve those involved in saw-milling and railways.

In 1898 the parish had a membership of 121, with six Elders and three Deacons (with three parish members also serving on the Deacon's Court). In 1956 there were 13 Elders and 16 Deacons. Woodlands is the only parish in the Presbytery to deny Eldership to women. In 2010 there were four Elders as members of a Parish Council.

Established in July 1864, with the ministry of Rev Thomas Alexander, who was followed by:

- 1887 Rev D. Dutton
- 1889 Rev H. Kelly
- 1894 Rev E. Bissett
- 1914 Rev G.H. Jupp
- 1918 Rev A.C. Wedderspoon
- 1921 Rev G.F. Cox
- 1925 Rev J.H. Robertson
- 1930 Rev G. Enwisk
- 1937 Rev N.F Sansom

- 1940 Rev G.E. Dallard
- 1946 Rev A Murdoch
- 1956 Rev W.G.B. Clark
- 1964 Rev J.A. Taggart
- 1970 Rev T.W.I. Lewis
- 1976 Rev Alan Kerr
- 1982 Rev Neville Burns
- 1987 Lay Supply

St Stephen's – 4 kms north of Invercargill city centre

Waikiwi district was initially served by Rev Stobo on his travels north of Invercargill. From 1869 it was served by Rev Bethune as part of the Myross Parish, then later it was under the oversight of the minister at Wallacetown. Initially, a church built for another denomination was used until the brick building on North Road was built in 1927. St. Stephen's Parish was established in 1890, with their first Minister being Rev Isaac Jolly who had arrived in 1887, then in 1890 Rev Robert Thornton. Waikiwi slowly developed as a suburb of Invercargill, and the parish was commissioned in 1890 with two Elders, nine Deacons and 112 members.

Ministers in following years were in 1898 Rev Dr James Cumming, 1914 Rev James Young and in 1919 Rev William Robertson, who also served the PSSA (Presbyterian Social Service Association) and was Presbytery Clerk. Then in 1939 Rev Leslie Rothwell and in 1945 Rev Thomas McDonald. In 1956, the parish had 12 Elders and 16 Deacons. The parish also incorporated a Sunday School Hall at Grasmere and a church at Makarewa, built during Rev Dr. Cumming's ministry. They utilised the services of retired Deaconess, Sr Dulcie Blick, from 1952 until her death in December 2006.

Then in 1959 Rev David Wilson, 1966 Rev Alan Morgan, and in 1975 they added Rev Russell Thew when the parish amalgamated with Makarewa, which had detached from St. Stephen's in 1960. In 1979, Rev David Jack was called but served only two years, as he then completed studies in England and returned as the Hospital Chaplain at Kew Hospital in Invercargill. He was followed by Rev Neal Whimp in 1981, Rev Michael Chappell in 1984 and Rev Alison Bell in 1990. She died in 1992 and was followed in 1994 by Rev Alan Matheson in a part time position. He was a member of the parish and also took on the role of Presbytery Clerk until he retired in 2002. The parish now has three Elders and a three-member Local Ministry Team, which includes a part-time Team Leader for a congregation of 40 members. The parish has since sold the Grasmere property and closed the church at Makarewa after providing services there on a shared basis for many years with All Saint's Anglican parish. Sacred Heart Catholic Church also serves this area of the city.

St Paul's, Invercargill – 1.5 kms north of city centre

When First Church's membership increased significantly, with Rev Bethune appointed in 1864 to oversee the process, it was proposed in the 1870s to form Second Church in Invercargill. Rev Alfred Arnot preached first at the Drill Hall and then in the Exchange Hall. The parish gained independence in 1875. The parish named St. Paul's included the areas of Avenal, Grasmere, Collingwood, Waihopai, Gladstone and West Plains. Many of the members transferred from First Church, with the first Sacrament of Holy Communion conducted by Rev Stobo. Rev Arnot resigned, and supply was provided by Rev Robert Ewen. After vigorous fundraising the building was opened in December 1876.

The parish started with 14 Elders, 15 Deacons and 276 members. Their first Minister was Rev James Paterson from Scotland, who attracted a strong following which necessitated two further increases in the seating in the church. He was followed in 1884 by Rev David Gordon and in 1888 by Rev George Lindsay, who was very active in work with children and youth. He oversaw the building of the Sunday School (now sold and demolished) and was for many years the District President of the Christian Endeavour Society. During his ministry the congregation was divided up when the parish at North Invercargill (Windsor) was established. He later became Moderator of the General Assembly. Ministers who followed were:

- 1911 Rev H.W. Burridge
- 1920 Rev Henry (Harry) Gilbert
- 1926 Rev Cecil Tocker
- 1954 Rev Ken McRae
- 1961 Rev Malcolm Highet
- 1969 Rev Robert Murphy
- 1973 Rev David Borne
- 1986 Rev Neil Cowie

Then after a long period of vacancy, the parish employed half-time Lay Worker Mr Alan Hawke, who in 2006 became part of a three-member Local Ministry Team, along with Mrs Deborah Clark and Dr Bruce McKercher. The parish also employed Deaconess Sr Heather Webster from 1967-1971. In 1956 the parish had 31 Elders and 22 Deacons. In 2010 there were five Elders, four Deacons and a membership of 20.

Winton – 40kms north of Invercargill

The first service of worship was held in Forest Hill by Rev Andrew Stobo, from First Church in Invercargill in 1867. Rev Alexander from Woodlands and Rev Stevens from Wallacetown provided ministry in the Winton and Forest Hill area until 1873 when the first church building was erected in Winton. The first minister Rev J.M. Thomson suffered from ill health, retired in 1878 and died in 1884. Much of his illness was aggravated by long days journeying around his parish in cold weather on muddy roads and farm tracks. The church building was destroyed by fire in 1878. Rev James Baird arrived in1879, and served for the following 23 years, retiring because of ill health in 1901, and then lived in Invercargill for a further 30 years. The Winton parish also provided for settlers in the Limehills and Oreti regions.

The parish was established in 1872, with Rev J. Thomson, who was followed by:

- 1879 Rev James Baird
- 1902 by Rev J.M. Simpson
- 1908 Rev R. Mackie
- 1918 Rev Arch. McNeur
- 1925 Rev H. Hogg
- 1931 Rev A.G. Gardiner
- 1937 Rev J. Newlands
- 1943 Rev H.W. Haigh
- 1950 Rev J.F. Rennie
- 1957 Rev H.S. MacLean
- 1974 Rev G.G. Roe
- 1984 Rev Richard S. Gray
- 1991 Rev Neville Jackson

It became part of Central Southland Presbyterian Parish (CSPP) in 1998. Church membership in 1898 was 85, with eight Elders and three Deacons. In 1956 there were six Elders and 14 Deacons.

Dipton parish – 60 kms north of Invercargill

This parish was originally served by ministers from Winton parish and then supplied as a Church Extension until Rev Kyd was inducted in 1893. Ministers often spent only a few years in the parish.

The Ministers who served in the parish were:

- 1892 Rev T.C. Guy (Supply)
- 1893 Rev W.A. Kyd
- 1897 Rev W.W. Brown (born in Southland)
- 1901 Rev J.T. Burrows
- 1906 Rev J. Davie
- 1911 Rev J. Miller
- 1914 Rev F.J. Tylee
- 1926 Rev J. Johnston
- 1938 Rev I.R. Polson
- 1944 Rev W. J. Wallace
- 1950 Rev C.L. Gosling
- 1959 Rev F.E. Slattery

The parish was amalgamated with Centre Bush in March 1972 and joined the Central Southland Parish in 1998.

Centre Bush – 50kms north of Invercargill

Due to the large area that Winton parish covered in the early 1900s, a further charge was established at Centre Bush in 1912 to include Otapiri and South Hillend. Services had been held in a barn since 1882, with a church building opening in 1884. Ministers who served Centre Bush parish were:

- 1913 Rev T. Knight (Supply)
- 1915 Rev R. Morgan
- 1923 Rev W.H. Norton
- 1929 Rev J. Cawley
- 1936 Rev J. MacGregor
- 1943 Rev L.K. Brown
- 1949 Rev C.A.G. McKenzie
- 1955 Rev R.W. Brown
- 1958 Rev K.T.F. Larsen
- 1963 Rev W.S. White
- 1970 Rev I.W. Haszard (amalgamated with Dipton 1972)
- 1983 Rev Ken Calvert
- 1990 Rev T. Timoteo
- 1992 Rev Colin Hegan

In 1998 Centre Bush joined the Central Southland Parish.

Taringatura (Lumsden) - 80kms north of Invercargill

This parish was established out of the Winton parish in 1885 following on from two Supply ministers. Their first minister was Rev W. Scorgie. Lumsden, with Balfour and Kingston (LBK) joined the Mataura Presbytery in 1971, with Mossburn joining Te Anau in 1960.

Forest Hill – 35 kms north-east of Invercargill

The parish of was established in 1894, following on from years of supply through Church Extension by home missionary Rev James McCaw. A church building had been erected in 1869, when it was part of the Winton parish. Rev George MacDonald was inducted to the charge in 1900.

Ministers who followed were:

- 1905 Rev A.K. Ross
- 1926 Rev D. McIntyre
- 1929 Rev J.C. Mill
  (died in office in 1939)
- 1940 Rev R.G. McKenzie
- 1950 Rev I.W. McIntosh
- 1969 Rev G. McInnes, joining
  with Hedgehope in 1977
- 1979 Rev Selwyn Yeoman
- 1988 Rev S. Mavaega

The parish closed in 1998 when it joined Central Southland Presbyterian Parish.

Hedgehope – 45 kms north-east of Invercargill

Worship services and a Sunday School commenced in 1900, provided by Rev E. Bissett from Woodlands. Land was acquired in 1903 for the church which was built in 1910. Seventeen ministers provided supply for short periods from 1910. Despite of attempts in 196, to merge the parish with neighbouring parishes, along with the dividing up of all the parishes north and east of Invercargill, the parish persisted on its own until 1977. Then the parish was amalgamated with Forest Hill.

Between 1915 and 1924, there were periods of fluctuating supply for the regions of Heddon Bush (informally attached to Nightcaps), Oreti and Drummond (traded with Limestone Plains for Fairfax and Lochiel). One notable supply minister was Mr Adam Hamilton, who gave up his training for Ordained Ministry to become a politician. (His bequest remains to this day as a provider of finance for Presbytery dispersal, initially for needy parishes, now re-assigned for Tertiary and Hospital Chaplaincies in Southland). Heddon Bush was variously attached to Winton and Centre Bush parishes until the establishment of the **Oreti Parish – 40kms north-west of Invercargill**, including Drummond and Heddon Bush.

Church buildings were erected at Drummond in 1900, Heddon Bush in 1907 and Oreti in 1912. The first minister inducted into this new charge was Rev J.S. Pate in 1925, followed by:

- 1930 Rev Andrew L. Miller
- 1935 Rev R. Dun
- 1939 Rev D.H. Hay
- 1944 Rev A.F. Sutherland
- 1951 Rev A.R. Scott
- 1956 Rev J. Mann
- 1964 Rev J.S. Thomson
- 1971 Rev B.M. Calder
- 1977 Rev Lesley Shaw
- 1982 Rev N.M. Daniela
- 1988 Rev Mary Huie-Jolly
- 1990 Rev Sherri Weinberg
- 1994 Rev Helen Wallis

In 1998 the parish became part of (CSPP) Central Southland Presbyterian Parish.

Limestone Plains – 25-40 kms northwest of Invercargill city centre

Rev James Clark was the Minister in Riverton in the 1860s. He was followed by Rev Charles Ross in 1871 after a period of supply by Mr Arnot, assisted by Mr Ewen who was responsible for Limestone Plains and the Waiau. Rev Ross was succeeded in 1877 by Rev James Cameron. When the Limestone Plains Parish was established in 1878, Rev Ewen's region of responsibility included Limestone Plains, Wrey's Bush, Otautau, the Waiau and Nightcaps, where coal was first mined in 1882. In 1879 the parish had four Elders, seven Deacons and 104 members.

In theory Rev Ewen ministered to all the settlers between Flint's Bush and Te Anau, having at one time 13 preaching places. They comprised a large area which he initially covered on foot and later on horseback. When gravelled roads were developed, he rode a buggy with pair of horses. His sermons, which often appeared in *The Southland Times*, were carefully prepared to cater to his mixed flock of farmers, flaxmillers, sawmillers and miners. He developed an outstanding church choir at Limestone Plains and was Moderator of Synod in 1891. He died suddenly in 1900 of a chill (at the Wallacetown manse) after 22 years of ministry.

A church was built at Isla Bank in 1881, after the manse (where services were held) was built in 1880. The original church building was replaced by a brick building named St. Cuthbert's in 1928.

Rev Ewen was followed by:

- 1900 Rev William Brown
- 1907 Rev Henry Barton
- 1912 Rev John Erwin
- 1916 Rev John Robertson
- 1921 Rev Andrew Smail
- 1925 Rev Walter Evans
- 1930 Rev George Mitchell
- 1945 Rev John Reilly
- 1951 Rev William Moore
- 1969 Rev Alfred Willoughby
- 1975 Rev Howard Smith (who became a Hospital Chaplain at Kew Hospital in 1979)
- 1982 Rev Kenneth Burnett (who provided supply during five years of vacancy)
- 1985 Rev David Smail
- 1992-1996 Rev Clive Haliday

The parish had a short ministry supply from Rev Jim Hunter in 1997 and lay pulpit supply since. Then from 1999 there was a part-time ministry supply by Rev Murray Marshall, LLM (Local Limited Ministry), during 2002–2004. The parish is now led by the Session and a Moderating Elder, overseen by an Interim Moderator. The parish has three preaching places, Waimatuku, Isla Bank and Thornbury, which they use in rotation, having decided in 1999 to discontinue the three services of worship held each Sunday (one in each venue). In 2010 there were five Elders on the Parish Council and 12 members of the parish.

St. Andrew's, Invercargill – 4 kms south of city centre

In the 1880s, the settlement of Invercargill was extending towards the south. Services were held in the Town Hall, then in the manse. From 1882, Rev Andrew Stobo provided a Supply Ministry. In 1890 South Invercargill was established as a Home Mission Station, and a church building seating 60 opened in 1894. Rev Stobo took sick leave and died in 1895. Supply was provided in 1898 by Rev L. Thompson, in 1899 as a Church Extension unit by Rev D.K. Fisher, who also developed a congregation at Tisbury, and in 1900 by Rev A.T. Thompson. In 1901 services were held at Appleby Hall and the church building and manse were moved to Tisbury to serve the community there and at Woodend.

Services at Appleby were supplied in 1902 by Rev J. Gilbert and Mr M. McLean, along with a supposed Congregational Minister from Chicago who was in fact something of a charlatan. With the parish of Knox Church being established in 1903, there were discussions by Presbytery about whether that should be the only parish in the south of Invercargill. But this was not adopted by St. Andrew's who continued using the Appleby Hall, which was then moved to Conon Street, as their church and Sunday School.

Supply to this Home Mission continued, (while protracted discussions continued over the issue of their relationship with Knox Church), in 1910 by Rev R. Morgan, 1913 by Rev E. Gardner, and 1916 by Rev W.W. Ewart, who was inducted into the full charge of the parish. The population of this area of Invercargill increased rapidly after the First World War and the parish was able to be self-supporting. Rev Ewart was followed in 1919 by Rev E. Gardner, who died in office in 1943, in 1944 by Rev K.S. Cree, and in 1944 by Rev G.P. Mitchell as a Locum Minister, while Rev Cree served overseas. The Youth Centre was built at this time.

The parish was served in 1952 by Rev George Johnston, in 1963 by Rev J.D.S. Moore, and in 1969 by Rev Bill Wallace. During this time deliberations continued regarding parish boundaries with St. David's and Knox, as residential areas of the city were developed and houses built. This growth also impacted on the Tisbury area. However, the families moving into the area were not wealthy and church finances suffered with the extra pastoral load. In 1977, Rev Wynford Davies came as Associate Minister for Rev Bill Wallace, who due to failing health became half-time, but also took on the role of Chaplain for Presbyterian Support Southland Association Rest Homes. Shortly after Rev Davies arrived however, Rev Wallace resigned.

Various discussions continued with regard to the parish boundaries and plans to cover the cost of a new manse and Assistant Ministers, which included assistance from the Adam Hamilton Fund (for 'needy' parishes).

Ministers since the 1980s have been:

- 1981 Rev Ian Hyslop
- 1984 Rev Andrew Norton (as Assistant Minister then as Associate Minister after his ordination) at the time of the parish extension into Carendon.
- 1987 Rev Neville Burns who retired in 2004
- 2005 Rev Derrick Hills, who resigned.
- 2006 Rev Dr. Cecil Kirk (Stated Supply from USA)
- 2007 Mr Nyalle Paris (half-time Lay Supply, then Ministry Intern)
- 2010 Rev Nyalle Paris

St. Andrew's parish had four Elders and eight members of the Deacon's Court with only three Deacons in 1891 and a membership of 45, then in 1956, 13 Elders and 16 Deacon's. In 2010, there were eight Elders and six Deacon's with a parish membership of 80.

Fortrose (Toitois) – 50 kms east of Invercargill

Fortrose township was established to serve the settlers in the Lower Mataura area and in particular the Toitois harbour into which the Mataura and Waimahaka rivers flow. Whalers and coastal steamers regular moored at the port. The community was initially served by Home Missioners based in **Waikawa** and Otara. The parish was established in 1883. The parish from time to time also included **Tokanui,** Seaward Downs, Waimahaka and **Mokoreta.**

The history of the Tokanui parish was a one of fluctuating boundaries, first established in 1895 as a Home Mission Station with Mr Blair providing supply, followed by very short-term supply by a number of home missioners. With the formation of the Mataura Presbytery in 1899, a reconfiguring of connection saw Mokoreta and Seaward Downs attached to Edendale in 1904 in the Mataura Presbytery, with Toitois (Fortrose) remaining with Southland through the railway link at Waimahaka. These arrangements continued until 1913 when Waikawa was separated from Mokoreta, which was joined with Redan and Wairekiki as a Home Mission Station, with Brydone (Waimumu) in 1935 and Edendale in the Mataura Presbytery in 1943.

In 1913 Waikawa was transferred to Southland Presbytery and continued to be supplied as a Home Mission Station. Even with the decline in viability of the port at Waikawa, the parish served a wide area of saw-milling reaching to the Chaslands, which later became part of the Catlins parish in the Clutha Presbytery. In the 1940s the parish again included Waikawa and Chaslands. This parish underwent many changes in its boundaries, going in and out of the Southland and Mataura Presbyteries and had many name changes. In the 1960s Tokanui and Fortrose were investigated and a merger brought about under the name of Toetoes which in 1972 became Toitois. In 1896, as part of the Lower Mataura parish Fortrose had three Elders and six Deacons, then in 1956, 12 Elders and 16 Deacons.

Ministers were:

- 1883 Rev J. Johnston
- 1904 Rev W. Findlay
- 1920 Rev D.D. Heggie
- 1925 Rev E.G. Evans
- 1934 Rev W.A. Carmichael
- 1940 Rev C. McCaskill
- 1945 Rev J.H. Thomson (Supply)
- 1948 Rev G.C.M. Angus
- 1956 Rev I. MacMillan
- 1961 Rev D.W. Pimm
- 1968 Rev Barry Doig
- 1975 Rev R.H. Wells
- 1978 Rev W.J. Orange, then after a period of Lay Supply,
- 1984 Rev Peter Cody
- 1985 Rev Russell Brass, (nine months)
- 1990 Keith Wilson (Lay Supply from Wallacetown)

In 2010, with Rev Wilson's resignation, and a membership of only ten, the parish linked with St. Andrew's, Invercargill.

Otautau / Waiono – 50-90 kms west north-west of Invercargill city centre

As already referred to, Otautau, Ohai, Nightcaps, Wairio and Opio were ministered to by Rev Robert Ewen who covered a very wide territory. When the parishes of Otautau, Nightcaps and Orawia, as well as Orepuki (now both part of the Waiau Valley parish), Waimatuku (Limestone Plains) and Waianawa (Wallacetown) were established, this lightened his load somewhat. Services had originally been held at the Strathmore, Birchwood and Otahu sheep stations until Otautau was surveyed and established. Services were subsequently held at the hotel and later still at the school. The church building was opened in 1890.

Nightcaps was developing as a mining centre, so the parish was divided from the Limestone Plains Parish, and in 1892 the parish was established at Otautau with Rev Alexander Macdonald, who had come from South America, in charge. There were eight Elders, 13 Deacons and 115 members. In 1900, a Church Extension charge was established for Nightcaps, Opio and Wairio, which also included South Hillend, Heddon Bush (from the Winton parish). Rev Macdonald was noted for his long ministry in Otautau of 33 years, dying five years after retiring. Later another stationing was made at Waiau, which became Merrivale and in 1916, became Orawia. The current church building in Otautau was opened in 1928. Otautau Parish became a Union parish, joining with the Methodist Church and in 1987 and joined with the Wairio parish. In 1956 the parish had seven Elders and 16 Deacons.

Ministers in Otautau were:

- 1925 Rev John Bickerstaff
- 1929 Rev William Howes
- 1938 Rev Harold Burnett
- 1949 Rev John Condie
- 1956 Rev Alec (Bill) Mudie
- 1963 Rev Roy McKenzie
- 1970 Rev Philip Brown
- 1977 Rev Alan Shaw
- 1985 Rev Doug Rogers (Methodist)
- 1990 Rev Stephen Lindsay

There followed a period of Lay Supply from Mrs Judith Day (Methodist), Student Supply in the Summer and a year's Lay ministry from Stephen Hurd in 2005, then a period of Pulpit Supply which continued when the parish joined the Southland Regional Resource Ministry in 2010.

A new parish was opened in **Nightcaps** in 1900, which called Rev Thomas Tait as its first minister, and in 1926 a church was built at **Ohai**, with Rev Thomas Campbell as the minister. Nightcaps, Wairio and Ohai had, over a period of 50 years, a history of short ministries, of between one and six years with as many as 13 vacancies in between. In 1929 there were two ministers, with one at Ohai and one at Nightcaps. In 1973, The Nightcaps, Wairio, Ohai Parish became a union parish called Waiono (Wai for Wairio, O for Ohai, N for Nightcaps and O for Opio) and amalgamated with Otautau in 1987. The churches at Wairio and Nightcaps have since been closed and the church buildings sold. Latterly the Union with the Methodist Church has been dissolved, and the Parish Council resigned at the 2012 AGM due to lack of personnel as office-bearers. Ohai and Otautau members then each formed a small committee of four people who oversee the day-to-day functions of each of their congregations, each of which has a worshipping congregation of 10 members. Rev Ivan Smith, retired and living in Nightcaps, conducted worship once a month throughout the year and for both the two services each month in the winter.

Waiau Valley – 80 kms west of Invercargill city centre

Waiau Valley Parish was formed in 1991 as an amalgamation of two parishes that had previous been four separate parishes, Merrivale-Waiau and Tuatapere-Orepuki, with Rev Ian Pimm as their Minister. In 1910 a 'sawmills mission' divided the area of Western Southland into Merrivale, Eastern Bush, Belmont, Feldwick and Orawia, to become the Orawia parish and Clifden and Tuatapere, while the Lilburn Valley made up the Tuatapere Parish. In 1868, gold was discovered at Orepuki and Round Hill (in the Riverton parish) so the population at Orepuki grew, with a large presence of Chinese miners at Round Hill. These miners had been served by Paul Ah Chin and then Mr Hugh Cowie who had been a missionary in Amoy. However, he did not speak Cantonese as the miners did, so Rev Alexander Don was sent to Canton to learn the language and returned to minister at Round Hill and later in Lawrence and Dunedin, continuing to maintain oversight of Chinese congregations in Otago and Southland. Rev Ross at Riverton visited when he could, at least quarterly, conducting the first service of Holy Communion in 1874. Mr William Nichol, who later became Rev Nichol, served at Orepuki for a year from 1874.

Ten years later, as the gold was running out, a Mr Carter was appointed to a parish that included Orepuki, Pahia, Round Hill and

Colac Bay (which was predominately Māori). He was followed in 1888 by Mr Hain, formerly an Elder and the Sunday School teacher at First Church in Invercargill, who went on to ordination a few years later. A church building was erected at Orepuki in 1890 with 60 members, and a session was formed in 1897, with Round Hill, Pahia and Colac Bay becoming Home Mission stations. Mr Hain was followed by:

- 1899 Rev George Roby
- 1911 Rev John Lopdell
- 1928 Rev Leonard Hodson
- 1930 Rev John Wylie
- 1933 Rev Angus Climie
- 1935 Rev Walter Humble
- 1937 Rev George Dallard
- 1939 Rev David (Jack) Martin

The parish was linked with Tuatapere in 1941. This parish was established in 1915, when farming and sawmilling had been established in the Waiau Valley, with six Elders and 13 Deacons. A church was built in 1917. Ministers were:

- 1913 Rev Robert McEwan
- 1918 Rev Robert Hill
- 1921 Rev Samuel Waddell
- 1927 Rev Albert Lion
- 1931 Rev David Campbell
- 1934 Rev James Thomson
- 1937 Rev Edgar Allison
- 1938 Rev Malcolm McFadgen
- 1949 Rev Henry Bartlett
- 1956 Rev Norman Sheat
- 1966 Rev Ivor Davies
- 1969 Rev Gordon Mackie
- 1967 Rev Kevin Ridley
- 1985 Rev Stuart Lange

The Waiau Parish was established in 1903 with the Rev George Mitchell, two Elders and four Deacons at Orawia. Two years later it was renamed as Merrivale Parish. Ministers who served there were:

- 1905 Rev Robert Robinson
- 1906 Rev Richard Morgan
- 1908 Rev George Falconer
- 1910 Rev John Johnston

Lay ministers served until 1915 when the parish was re-named again as Orawia. The following 36 years saw 15 ministers serve there. The longest serving remained for four years, while most were for just one or two years at a time. In 1953, under the charge of Rev Allison, the parish was re-named again as Merrivale-Waiau. In 1956 there were seven Elders and seven Deacons. Ministers who served this new parish were:

- 1958 Rev Dallas Clark
- 1967 Rev James Jones
- 1971 Rev Wallace Murray
- 1979 Rev Tame (Tom) Hawea
- 1988 Rev James Cullingford
- 1990 Rev Stuart Lange and Rev Ian Pimm

In 1997, the Waiau Valley Parish was established from the merger of Merrivale-Waiau and Tuatapere-Orepuki, based at Tuatapere, with services held each Sunday at Tuatapere and Orawia. From 2000-2005, Mrs Sue Hogbin provided lay ministry supply. Short terms of ministry supply were provided by ministers from USA and Australia, using the manse as a base for travel throughout the country. Ministers included:

- 2005 Rev Bob Lantz from USA
- 2006 Mr Peter and Mrs Caroline Horrell
- 2006 Mr Laurie and Mrs Jeanette Parkinson
- July-November 2009 Mr Eddie and Mrs Nola Frost
- March-June 2010 Mr Dennis and Mrs Phyllis Crookes from Australia

The church buildings at Eastern Bush and Orawia were sold in 2002. Since 2008 the parish has been led by a Ministry Team of six Elders on Session, led by a Moderating Elder, with oversight from the Resource Ministers of the Southland Regional Resource Ministry.

Oteramika / Kennington – 5 kms east of Invercargill

Originally part of the Long Bush Oteramika Parish, the region was supplied by the Woodlands parish by:

- 1891 Rev James McCaw
- 1895 Rev W.P. Brown
- 1897 Rev R. Gardner
- 1899 Rev J. Dickie

With the establishment of the parish of Oteramika in 1900, the ministers inducted to the charge were:

- 1900 Rev C.A. Gray
- 1905 Rev E.J. Carter
- 1910 Rev N.D. Nicholson
- 1912 Rev J. McGregor
- 1917 Rev W.R. Hume
- 1922 Rev J.A. Reilly
- 1927 Rev D. McColl

The parish was then amalgamated in 1936 with the recently established Kennington parish, which also included the Rimu area. In 1923 the parish had four Elders and four Deacons. In 1956 the Kennington parish had 16 Elders and 12 Deacons.

In 1985, when the parish was vacant the question arose again of the boundaries for the Oteramika / Kennington (OK) parish. The proposals put to the parish gave them three options: for Kennington to join Richmond Grove and Oteramika to re-join Woodlands, to stay as they were or for the OK Parish to join Woodlands. The vote was in favour of staying the same, so no change was made and a new manse was built to replace the previous manse. With diminishing membership over recent years, the parish has from time-to-time discussions had with neighbouring parishes about possible amalgamations. The parish has been well served for many years by their Interim Moderator, Rev Ken Calvert who resides in the area.

In 2010 the parish has a Parish Council with 12 members, six of whom are Elders. The membership is 20.

Kennington parish was formed in 1924. The minsters who served were:

- 1924 Rev J.H. Thompson
- 1943 Rev F.R. Belmer
- 1948 Rev J.B. Powell
- 1954 Rev T.G. Calder
- 1967 Rev C. MacCaskill
- 1970 Rev Chris Nichol
- 1974 Rev D.R. Reid
- 1986 Rev M. Lau'ese

From 1993 various supply ministers and lay preachers served the parish.

Knox, Invercargill – 1.5 kms south east of the city centre

The establishment of Knox Church in Appleby, on the corner of Ness and Balmoral Streets in 1903, to serve South Invercargill, was not supported by the members of St. Andrew's, who continued to meet in the Appleby Hall. It was proposed that St. Andrew's become a Home Mission of Knox, with Elders and Deacons being on Knox Session and Deacon's Court, with the Knox Minister living in the St. Andrew's manse ,while a manse was being built for Knox Church. The situation remained unsatisfactory so, in January 1905, St. Andrew's was disjoined from Knox.

The first minister was Rev F.W. Dunlop who was ordained and inducted to the charge in January 1904. The building was erected in 1914 during the time of Rev J.W. Shaw who left in 1915 to serve in the war. He was followed by Rev Hector Maclean. In 1921 Rev John Chisholm commenced an 18 year tenure during which time the parish extended east, to set up a Home Mission in Centre Street, Georgetown. In 1939 Rev A. Kernohan arrived and found the duplication of services, Sunday School and youth activities necessitated the need to relocate the parish to one site in Georgetown. The Earn Street manse was sold and 'Ellesland' the former home of Captain Elles was purchased along with its large grounds, which became the site of the new Knox Church, in Pomona Street.

Ministers who followed were:

- 1954 Rev A.R. Scott
- 1966 Rev M.N. Dickey
- 1972 Rev T.D. Phillipps
- 1982 Rev J. McKinley

Rev McKinley resigned in 1999 to become the Principal of an Invercargill branch of the New Zealand Bible College, based in the Sunday School rooms and manse at Knox Church. In 2005, a Local Ministry Team made up of Mr Noel Spiers, Mrs Nardia Livingstone and Mrs Pam Strang, was commissioned to provide ministry for the parish. The Ministry Team has been expanded over the years to include most of the parish elders who also serve as members of the Parish Council. In 1905 there were six Elders on Session and five Deacons on the Management Committee. In 1956 there were 13 Elders and 19 Deacons. Parish membership has declined considerably over the years, to a small number of members, with seven members on the Parish Council.

Knox Church has for many years had both Boys' and Girls' Brigade companies ably lead by a team of officers, mostly provided by members of the parish. This significant outreach brought many girls and boys from the local community into contact with the Church.

North Invercargill – 5 kms north east of city centre

The Church was opened as a Branch Church of St. Paul's parish in 1905. From 1907, Ministry Supply was provided by Rev H. Clark with other lay preachers and ministry students until 1911. After the loss of its building from fire, the parish was established as a full charge in 1914 with Rev J. Collie. In 1916, a new church building opened on the corner of Windsor and Bourke Streets. In 1914 there were three Elders and seven Deacons.

Rev W. Tanner followed in 1926, with a new larger building opening in 1928. Then, after considerable growth in the population of the parish, he was followed in 1939 by Rev H. Graham, and in 1947 by Rev A.D. Robertson, during whose time the need was identified to form a parish in the suburb of Waverley, with the peak of the North Church membership at 613 members. In 1956 there were 34 Elders and 20 Deacons.

Ministers thereafter were:

- 1959 Rev R.S. Anderson
- 1963 Rev A.J. Huston
- 1968 Rev Michael J. Thawley (later to become Assembly Moderator 2000-2002)
- 1971 Rev M.N. Fink Rev B Wendelborn and Rev Norma Graves (Associate Ministers)

- 1976 Rev J.R. Brinsley
- 1982 Rev A.M. Martin
- 1987 Rev G.G. Ashton
- 1988 Rev W. Sweets (Supply from USA)
- 1990 Rev Derrick Hills (Associates)
- 1998 Rev Alistair Taylor

Rev Taylor oversaw the amalgamation with Waverley Parish to form Windsor Community Church (Presbyterian).

Te Anau – 180 kms north west of Invercargill

Established in 1962, the parish was served by:

- 1962 Rev E.J. Miller
- 1966 Rev Ian Galloway
- 1977 Rev R.G. Oates
- 1981 Rev Ian Haszard
- 1986 Rev A.M. Martin, followed by many periods of Supply Ministry.
- 2000 Rev Karl Lamb (initially Summer Supply then ordained and inducted as Locally Ordained Minister)
- 2005 Rev Karl Lamb (Nationally Ordained Minister).

In 2010 with a membership of 100, there were six Elders and six Deacons.

Richmond Grove – 3 kms north east of city centre

Established in 1952 as an offshoot of First Church, gifting approximately 100 members, with ten Elders and nine Deacons under the charge of Rev James N. Reid, who was followed by:

- 1963 Rev G.A. Hay
- 1973 Rev T.E. Millar
- 1978 Rev Noel Butler
- 1989 Rev Barry Ayers
- 2004 Mr Tony Dawson, Lay Supply, who was ordained as a Locally Ordained Minister in 2009

The parish had six Elders, four Deacons and 40 members in 2010.

Waverley – 8 kms north-east of Invercargill city centre

Established in 1955, as a church extension into the north-east development of Glengarry, Waverley and Rosedale, with 6 Elders and 6 Deacons. Ministers who served were:

- 1955 Rev R. Wilson
- 1965 Rev A. McG. Kirkwood
- 1969 Rev L.J. Reid
- 1977 Rev A. Ron Townsend
- 1999 Rev David Gordon

A period of vacancy followed in 2002, during which the decision was made to close the parish, sell the buildings and amalgamate with

North Invercargill Church to form Windsor Community Church (Presbyterian).

St. David's – 4 kms south east of city centre

Set up as a parish in 1957 and officially opened in 1958 as an outreach of First Church on the corner of Regent and White Streets, in the newly established suburb of Newfield, incorporating Hawthorndale. Ministers who served were:

- 1957 Rev A.C. Herron
- 1962 Rev J.A. Mitchell
- 1967 Rev R. McD. Durham (Stated Supply then inducted as Minister in 1970)
- 1972 Rev P.R. Wishart
- 1980 Rev Murray Talbot
- 1990 Rev F. Fransham
- 2003 Rev Ian Crawford, following a period of vacancy, (Summer Supply)

Rev Crawford was then Ordained (Locally Ordained Minister) and inducted in 2005, until 2010 when the parish was again Vacant.

The parish had in 2010, six Elders on Session and four Deacons and two members on the Board of Management with a membership of 40.

Mossburn – 100 kms north of Invercargill city centre

This parish for a long time was linked with Te Anau and was first called Mararoa. The parishes of Te Anau and Mossburn, which had separated from Lumsden, both separated from Taringatura Parish. Ministers at Mossburn were:

- 1962 Rev Evan Miller
- 1966 Rev Ian Galloway
- 1977 Rev Roger Oates
- 1981 Rev Ian Haszard
- 1986 Rev Anthony (Tony) Martin
- 1990-1992 Mr Harry Kemp

Since then, the parish has been served for very short periods by Stated Supply and Lay Ministry. Mossburn enjoyed a settled period of Lay Supply with Mr Chris Waples, and then in July 1997 Mossburn separated from Te Anau, with Lay Supply from Mr Trevor Parkinson 2001-2004 and Mr David Kimpton in 2004, then Mr Brian Gallagher in July 2005.

However, Presbytery had not been properly informed or involved in Mr Gallagher's employment. When this appointment became unsatisfactory, Presbytery had to step in and remedy the situation. In 2007, the Session resigned, a Commissioner was appointed and two Presbytery Elders from Winton were appointed to a temporary Church Council called the Interim Management Team. A new Parish Council and Local Ministry Team were commissioned in 2008 prior to the parish joining the Southland Regional Resource Ministry.

The parish is still acutely aware of the mistakes they have made which have taken a long time to remedy, and there are still repercussions that arise from time to time. This is a salient lesson to be learned by parishes that are left to their own devices without oversight by an appropriate Minister appointed by Presbytery. New Elders have recently been ordained at Mossburn, and the parish is endeavouring to connect with the community more by forging links with the Catholic and Anglican congregations, both of which are also very small groups of residents. Rev Heather Kennedy oversees the Leadership Team as their Resource Minister. In 2010 the parish had three Elders, two Elders Emeriti, two Parish Councillors and 30 members.

Otatara Community Church – 5 kms west of Invercargill city centre

Discussions between St. Paul's Church and the Methodist Church began in 1963 regarding a co-operation at Otatara. In 1977 a Deed of Agreement was finally in place. In 1979 an amended agreement was reached and the Ruru Avenue Methodist Hall was moved to Oreti Street in Otatara and altered for worship purposes, with plans in mind to extend the building once additional land was bought. Building projects have been undertaken, with the addition of a hall/ Sunday School room. Lay supply was provided by Steve Harrex, from 2000.

Pacific Island Church, Invercargill – 2 kms south of city centre

With the arrival of Pacific Islanders in Invercargill, predominately to work in the Freezing Works at Bluff, a Presbyterian Parish for Pacific Islanders was established in 1969. Ministers were in 1969 Rev Vaomu Lima, in 1975 Rev Aotofaga Lemuelu, who advised and served as Chaplain for Pacific Islanders in their workplaces, and in 1985 Rev Matatia Erika, who also offered translation in judicial hearings and a work training scheme for Pacific Islanders with limited English. He was also member of the Advisory Committee for the Ministry of Pacific Island Affairs and the Pacific Island representative for the Mission Resource Board.

The Cook Island and Samoan groups separated. Rev Kimi Henry (Local Limited Ministry) LLM (Cook Island), served the Cook Islanders worshipping at Clarendon Presbyterian Church (previously planted by St. Andrew's parish as an outreach to Tiwai Smelter employees who lived in Clarendon), until it was closed, then sold to the Manaia Cultural Trust. The Cook Island PIC then joined St. Andrew's parish and continues to have Cook Island language services provided by Rev Tau Ben Unu from Mataura.

The PIC (Samoan) parish continued worshipping at the Ness Street property with Rev Iona Sua LLM (Samoan) until the parish was closed in 2010, with the decommission of their building on the corner of Balmoral and Ness Street, formerly the Knox Church building. The six Members of the parish (including three Deacons, i.e. PIC Elders) and members of their extended families then chose to worship with members of First Church and started plans towards incorporation.

Central Southland Presbyterian Parish

This parish was established in 1998 as an amalgamation of Winton, Dipton, Oreti, Drummond and Centre Bush Parishes. Initially with the Ministers from Winton and Centre Bush, Rev Neville Jackson (Associate) who retired in 2008, and Rev Donald Hegan (Associate) who resigned in 2005, then in 2007 with Rev Tekura Wilding (Associate) and following in 2009 with Rev Cherry Thompson (Associate). In 2010 there were 12 Elders and 12 Deacons and 300 members.

Windsor Community Church (Presbyterian) – 5 kms north-east of Invercargill city centre

This parish was established in 2002 as an amalgamation of Waverley and North Invercargill Parishes. This process was carried out while

Rev Alistair Taylor was the minister at North Presbyterian Church and following his retirement in 2008. In 2009 Rev Ian Crawford a Locally Ordained Minister, as the Interim Moderator provided two years Stated Supply. The parish also employs a full-time Youth Worker, a Children and Families Worker, a Pastor for Elderly and full-time office staff. The parish had a membership 350 with 26 Elders and 15 Deacons in 2010.

Summary

From the very beginning, with the arrival of missionaries and the translation of the Bible into a written form of Māori, to the spreading of the gospel to the furthest corners of New Zealand and the establishment of the Presbyterian Church by the Free Church of Scotland in Otago and Southland, there was a wholehearted desire to share the Good News with everyone in this new country. The intentional establishment of parishes throughout the Otago and Southland regions continues to this day in one form or another. However, though historically it was an accepted practice to establish parishes or close them or merge them with others depending on need or changes in the make-up of the community, that now seems very difficult to undertake.

Over the years, boundaries have been constantly changed, but with the decision to not observe parish boundaries, membership has become more fluid and parishes tend to look to history to lead their decisions when considering mergers and amalgamations. Looking back on their histories may encourage parishes to follow early examples and see if there are ways where they can work together to better serve their communities. Their needs and circumstances have changed and many are no longer the viable, strong and well-attended independent parishes they were in the past. This has been the focus of the suggestions for change and ideas for a new way of being church in Southland over the years 1990-2010. The following chapter looks at some of the options that have been explored.

Chapter 2 – Southland Presbytery 1865-1990

In the early 1860s three ministers were ordained into charges at Invercargill, Riverton and Woodlands, therefore the Otago Presbytery formed the Southland Presbytery on 5 May 1865, with Rev Stobo as the first Moderator. Wallacetown was also constituted as a charge at that time with Rev Stevens as the minister, and the Presbytery of Mataura was formed in 1891 seated in Gore, with the Otago Presbytery changing its name to Dunedin Presbytery. This region, south of the Waitaki River remained connected to the Free Church of Scotland, whereas the (misnamed) Presbyterian Church (of the rest) of New Zealand was connected to the Church of Scotland until the southern presbyteries and the Synod of Otago and Southland joined in the 'union of incorporation' with the northern region in 1901.

1990-2010

In 1990 it was recorded that there were 26 parishes in Southland Presbytery with 28 Ordained Ministers, which included the Hospital Chaplain and the Presbyterian Support Southland Chaplain for Rest Homes. North Invercargill Presbyterian parish had two ministers and Oban parish was without a minister.

The Presbytery was made up of a Commissioner (Ordained Minister) and an Elder from each parish in Southland, a total of 54 members and a Presbytery Clerk who was employed part-time. A Moderator was elected every two years from the membership. Each November the membership of the Committees of Presbytery was appointed by the Standing Committee which included the Moderator, the Clerk and the Chairs of the Committees.

The Committees of Presbytery were, the:

- Business (and Pastoral) Committee
- Ministry Committee
- Parish Mission Committee
- Mission Overseas Committee

- Public Questions Committee
- Property Committee, and
- Finance Committee.

The Association of Presbytery Women (APW), the Joint Regional Committee (JRC) of Co-operating Ventures and the Southland Presbyterian Youth (SPY) Committee were also represented at presbytery meetings and tabled reports to presbytery. Occasionally, other committees were formed for specific reasons, such as the Statistics Committee and the Standing Committee. All members of presbytery were also on at least one committee, most of which met every month and reported to presbytery meetings.

Presbytery meetings were held every month, other than January. Monthly meetings at First Church commenced at 5.30pm with greetings and devotions from the Moderator. Formal business was undertaken, then a meal was provided. The meeting continued after tea, often past 10pm, and was followed by a time of prayer. Three Orders of the Day were also included – one before the break for tea and two afterwards. These were of a varied nature, but were usually: a report from a parish, a local organisation, such as Presbyterian Support Southland Association (PSSA) or a Study Leave report. They were reasonably short and had no business actions assigned to them. From 1990 to 2000 all Presbytery meetings were held at First Church in Central Hall with the meal catered for by women from Knox Church. Parishes in turn would be the hosts, providing worship and music content.

Presbytery appointed Interim Moderators to a parish when it became vacant. There was always a Presbytery Representative on the Nomination Board established in a parish to fill a vacancy. Presbytery also appointed five members (Ministers and Elders) to five Quinquennial Visitation Committees each year, to undertake the five-yearly visits to parishes, to review their ministry, their buildings and their mission.

Presbytery also appointed representatives to:

- Presbyterian Support Southland Association (PSSA)
- Joint Regional Committee (JRC)

- Inter-Church Trade and Industry Mission (ITIM) Chaplaincy
- Churches Education Commission "Bible In Schools" (CEC)
- Southland Tertiary Charitable Trust Board (STCCTB), after 2001, and the
- Committees of the Synod of Otago and Southland.

Reports from these organisations were also recorded in the presbytery minutes. Any concerns raised were referred to the appropriate committees to discuss and bring to Presbytery for action.

Committees of Presbytery

Standing Committee

This committee was formed each year to appoint those ministers and elders who were members of presbytery, to each of the committees of presbytery.

Presbytery Executive

The Executive was made up of the Moderator, the Deputy Moderator (or Moderator-Elect), the Clerk of Presbytery and the Convenors of all Presbytery Committees. Their role was to receive reports from the committees, oversee the duties of the committees and to work together on the various special projects of presbytery, such as a training seminar, the visit of dignitaries or mission initiatives. Along with members of the Ministry committee, the Executive oversaw the Ordination and/or Induction of Ministers, the Commissioning of Officers of Presbytery, and appointed members to the Student Assessment Committee as and when required to assess candidate's sense of call to Ordained Ministry.

Business

This committee arranged the agenda and order of business for presbytery meetings.

The frequency of meetings was often discussed and various timeframes were trialled.

Orders of the Day also included invited representatives of:

- the Prison, Hospital and Tertiary Chaplaincies,
- Presbyterian Support Chaplain
- Christian Education Commission (Bible in Schools)
- Girls' and Boys' Brigades
- Missionaries on furlough
- visiting Ministers from abroad
- local dignitaries, and
- members of PCANZ with Assembly positions.

In 1999, the decision to cease having meetings at First Church saw the venue moved around the parishes of the Southland Presbytery with the host parish providing the meal, worship and music content.

Ministry and Pastoral Care

The main responsibility of this committee was to provide pastoral care and administrative oversight of ministers in parishes and chaplaincies. This committee was responsible for the administration of Calls to ministers to fill vacancies, resignations, retirements, sick leave, Study Leave and Professional Development. Pastoral care of ministers, review of minister's performance, welcoming and the farewells for ministers were also tasks overseen by this committee. Each minister who undertook a period of Study Leave was required to present a report on their leave at a presbytery meeting. A record was kept by the Presbytery Clerk of all leave taken and those who had not taken Study Leave were required to do so as part of their Professional Development commitment.

Parish Mission

Members of this committee were responsible for the parish Quinquennial Visitation programme and for providing interesting missional options for parishes to consider implementing in order to potentiate their mission objectives. Various programmes were accessed and provided by trained presenters.

In 1998 a Mission Audit was undertaken asking four main questions:

- Mission Statement: Do all parishes know their mission statement? How is it implemented?
- If the Congregation vanished tomorrow, how would the community in which you are set, be poorer? Who would notice you were gone? What would be needed to replace your ministry in the community?
- What innovative ideas have you implemented in the past five years? Do they enhance, improve or enrich your community?
- What are the crisis points in your community?

The 'Inspiration Day' held in mid-1998 found that most parishes had been too comfortable for too long, making the need for change hard to face. There could be a huge opportunity for mission and ministry when there are no buildings or money. Sunday should not be the only worship slot, mid-week worship works as well.

Therefore – 'What are the opportunities (beyond our traditional mind-sets and expectations) for **our** congregation in **our** community?

Mission Overseas and Public Questions

This committee formed in 1990 connected with Southland missionaries overseas and also discussed contentious topical issues.

Many of the members of this committee were frequently in contact with Southlanders serving in missionary positions overseas. Reports on their activities were shared at Presbytery meetings. When the internet became more widely used, correspondence with missionaries became more intimate and immediate, meaning that members of presbytery could be in touch on a personal basis and not so reliant on information from this committee.

Missionaries supported by Southland Parishes and Southland APW were:

Prior to 2000
- Lynette Bay, Luke Bridge, Eddy Cheng, Dr Rosemary Ayers and Emma Halsted (Kapsower Hospital).
- Natalie Williamson (AIM Uganda).
- Florence Hamilton, Rev Doreen Riddell (Jaghadri, North India).
- David and Helen Dunn, Callum and Fiona McKinley (Taiwan), and
- Dorothy Price.

2000-2010

- Alison Loan (Invercargill) in Fujiara, United Arab Emirates with the Evangelical Presbyterian Missionary Fellowship.
- Dianne and Jim Young (Southland and Cromwell), in Lilongwe, Malawi with Service in Mission (SIM).
- Russell (Winton) and Mirelle Cross in Chad with African Inland Mission (AIM).
- Lindsay King (Te Anau) in China with Interserve.
- Maree Scully in New Delhi, then South Africa.
- Kerry and David Vercade in Bangladesh.
- Neal and Jill Whimp (nee Sutton), in Vanuatu.
- John and Elizabeth Thompson in Jigga-jigga and Addis Ababa, Ethiopia.
- Jim and Helen Harrington in Burkina Faso.
- Wallace and Colleen Searle in Peru.
- Chris and Helen Cowie (and Paul) with SIM
- Nurse Elizabeth Tisch in Zambia.

During the 1990s and into the new millennium there were many issues in the church and society that were monitored by this committee. The progress of national debates, government decisions, Assembly decisions and local areas of concern were reported on by this committee. Again, with easy access to information and the ability to communicate by email, the role of this committee was not so important and membership was not sustained.

Property and Finance

This committee met monthly to receive applications from parishes for any matters related to property and applications for funding for projects, as well as managing the finances of presbytery. During the 1990s, with the changes in the number of parishes and ministers, some parishes divested themselves of excess property, such as Sunday School halls, manses and buildings that were no longer fit for purpose.

The new millennium also provided a lot of work for the Property and Finance Committee with applications to the Synod of Otago and Southland for major building projects. These including joining buildings together with appropriate attachments and the refurbishment of existing buildings in both the Central Southland Presbyterian Parish (CSPP) and North Presbyterian Parish as it become the Windsor Community Parish (Presbyterian) after merging with Waverley Presbyterian Parish.

In a Building report at the time of the Presbytery Quinquennial visitation in May 2000 it was stated that the buildings at Windsor were used by a large number of people both from within the church and also the community. The report went on to say:

"Of more pressing concern regarding the buildings is their suitability to ministry and mission in the 21st century. In a previous Visitation Report it was commented that the buildings were purpose built for a bygone era. The size of the halls was limiting some of the activities especially school holiday programmes, the location of toilets raised safety issues for hall users, and in this day and age the community is attracted by buildings that invite people to enter and take part in the activities being offered." This motivated a small group of people to meet informally to consider the following – do the existing buildings meet the present needs of the church and community and those in the future? If we do need to make changes, can we "tweak" the existing buildings or should we be looking at a major project? The latter option was taken and from then on we added more people to the Site Development Committee and engaged architect Neil McDowell from our congregation to start working on various plan options. The congregation was asked to submit ideas and all the hall user groups were surveyed with a wide variety of questions because we wanted to try and fulfil as many of the requests as were practical.

There were also discussions with the Building Committee of Presbytery and we kept our neighbouring parishes of St Paul's and Waverley informed of our plans. The committee had decided that for such a large project to be successful and achievable it would have to be broken down into stages. All along we consulted and informed the congregation and were pleased with the encouragement from them, despite the fact that there was going to have to be a large financial commitment from them. We were very conscious of God's hand being in all of our planning and preparation. In January 2003 work began on the first stage – the complete rebuild of the kitchen. We now have a registered first-class facility which is a joy to work in. Stage 2 which consisted of a new hall, new and enlarged church foyer and connecting passageway to link the halls and church was the next target. To enable this to come to fruition we owe a huge debt of gratitude to the Synod of Otago and Southland who allocated us grants. Along with the money we had in hand and the commitment of, and ongoing fundraising efforts of our own parishioners we were able to let the contract for work to start in July 2004. Mr Eric Russell turned the first sod and from then on the contractor Mr Alan Gieseg and his team of men worked steadily until March 2005 when the building was finished. A large congregation celebrated the official opening when the Rev Dr Simon Rae, Moderator of the Southland Presbytery, led the service and unveiled a special plaque opening the new additions.

The large auditorium was named the "Jubilee Hall" – aptly named as the year 2005 is the 100th anniversary of the beginning of the North Invercargill Presbyterian parish. We now have a wonderful asset for the benefit of church users and the community with up-to-date technology available for a whole range of activities from social functions to seminars, to concerts, and weddings and everything else in between. But we are not finished! The next stage being planned now is a new toilet block including a shower and toilet for the disabled. We hope that in a few months' time we will have sufficient funding to get under way with that.

There are still some parts of the old hall which need refurbishing and there has also been discussion about new church offices but that is probably something to be considered in the distant future. In the meantime, we praise God for his wonderful provision. The final stage of our church redevelopment was completed and opened by Mr Fergus Sime (moderator of Synod of Otago and Southland) on 23rd Nov 2008."

Southland Connections

Various sub-committees and agencies were represented at Presbytery Meetings and provided reports from meetings, parishes and organisations.

Joint Regional Council – JRC

The Southland Joint Regional Council was the local committee of the Uniting Congregations of Aotearoa New Zealand (UCANZ). The committee was made up of two representatives of the Co-operating

Photographs

Current and previous First Church Ministers:
(standing) Rev Dr Simon Rae, Rev Brian Williscroft,
Rev Richard Gray, Rev Heather Kennedy,
(seated) Rev Dr Bob Eyles and Rev Crawford Madill
at First Church 150th Celebrations in 2010 (see page 12)

Linked Central Southland Presbyterian Parish building **(see pages 47-48)**

Windsor linking spaces (see pages 47-48)

St Paul's Sunday School Hall sold in 2001 (see page 20)

Southland APW graphic representation
displayed at the National Conference 2008 (see page 53)

Symbols of Ministry presented at the Induction Service (see page 69)

A Time of Change

First Presbyterian Church, Invercargill – 2004 (see page 12)

Centennial of Oban Presbyterian Church on Stewart Island – August 2004
(see page 11)

Ventures in the Southland Presbytery region and a representative of the three Partner denominations. The parishes represented were Bluff Co-operating Parish (Anglican, Methodist and Presbyterian), Otatara Community Church, Otautau Waiono Union Parish and Riverton Union Parish (all Methodist and Presbyterian).

The JRC met regularly and shared parish news, ministry matters and information from the UCANZ National Standing Committee. Members were invited to attend Presbytery, Methodist Synod and Anglican Diocesan events and the chairperson usually attended Standing Committee meetings held in Wellington. After the Otautau/Waiono Parish dissolved their union and became a Presbyterian parish, attendance at JRC meetings was erratic and it was decided to cease meeting, relying on UCANZ to administer it from the National Office and for members to be resourced by their partner of oversight.

Association of Presbyterian Women – APW

Throughout the 1990s most parishes in Southland Presbytery had a branch of the Association of Presbyterian Women, in whose activities many women in the parish took part. Meetings were held monthly and followed a usual pattern of devotions, correspondence, financial report, general business and a guest speaker or activity. Most branches supported the fundraising for the Annual Mission Project of APW and MWF (Methodist Women's Fellowship) and fundraising for local projects such as: Prison, Tertiary and Hospital Chaplaincies, CEC (Bible in Schools and School Chaplains), PSS (Presbyterian Support Southland) and other charities, as well as supporting Overseas Missionaries and Mission organisations, such as 'Mission and Service.'

Each branch was represented by two members on the Southland Presbyterial, who met regularly, published monthly newsletters, organised events and provided two elders for presbytery meetings, as well as sending two office-bearers to the annual APW Conference. Southland Presbyterial also provided members for the National Committee of APW for a term of office.

Over the years, as members of congregations aged, so did the members of APW. Younger women were working and attended church and

APW meetings as and when they were able. It became more difficult to find women capable and available to take on leadership roles in parishes and as parish numbers declined, the same occurred with APW. This was particularly so in rural parishes and smaller city parishes. Presbyterial meetings and event attendance declined and were held less frequently. This situation was not unique to Southland, as was discussed at the APW Annual Conferences and in Consultation documents, under the title of 'Growing Into Change' which included possibilities for the future of APW.

At the conference held in Feilding in 2008 it was decided to change the name of APW to PWANZ – Presbyterian Women Aotearoa New Zealand. This was a culmination of much discussion and identification of realities and what could be achieved in a new model. The driving force for change was the realisation that the reason for the formation of the PWMU (Presbyterian Women's Missionary Union) and the change to APW, was now superseded by the ordination of women as Elders and Ministers of Word and Sacrament, the changing presence of missionary work within parishes and overseas and the role of women in regional and national leadership in the church.

Southland Presbyterian Youth – SPY

This committee functioned mostly in the 1990s and saw the oversight of the Youth Camp at Taringatura and planned camps and various youth activities, youth training weekends, Easter Camps and youth worship services, balls and dances across the Presbytery. The membership was made up of representatives from parishes with Youth Groups, and Youth Pastors. For a while presbytery also employed a Youth Worker who liaised with parishes and helped organise and lead youth activities.

Over the years the responsibility for the oversight of the Taringatura Youth Camp became quite a large commitment, as repairs, renovation, maintenance, such as painting, were constantly needed. The sale of the property was considered as an option to ease the load.

Chapter 3 – Looking to the Future

Parish Mission Consultant

In 1993, a need was identified by the Ministry Committee of Southland Presbytery for a "Parish Mission Consultant" to be employed by the presbytery at one third of stipend to work for Presbytery Committees, Special Committees and Commissions, Quinquennial Visitations to provide Resource Advice, planning assistance and to be called upon in crisis situations.

The Parish Mission Consultant was charged with the duty of delivering the mission packages: From Maintenance to Mission, Gossiping the Gospel, Four Faces of Mission, Who Ministers Where? and Growth Evangelism projects to encourage members of the parishes to actively undertake these projects, to suggest initiatives and to provide links for parishes as they seek to fulfil their mission.

This position was advertised in Presbytery Notices in November 1993, following appendices 3i, 3ii and 3iii on the need for a Parish Mission Consultant. These appendices drew a comparison between a Consultancy and the role of a Director/Supervisor, gave a list of consultancy type of work that was in hand or had been requested by parishes and also the presbytery tasks that would be undertaken by the successful candidate. Rev Ron Townsend was the only applicant for the job, and the Board of Nomination agreed that he was suitable for the role, to commence in March 1994.

The Presbytery applied for funding for the position from the Synod of Otago and Southland to the tune of $5,700, which included a travel allowance of 763km per annum, with parishes that used his services paying the travel costs for his visits. However, it is unclear whether Rev Townsend ever really undertook the job, as there are no further references to the position, and there are no reports to Presbytery from this Parish Mission Consultant on the work being undertaken.

Presbytery minutes record that Rev Townsend tendered his resignation in May 1994, citing a lack of confidence in presbytery, but the resignation was withdrawn after mediation. Funding was provided for the consultant's role by the Synod of Otago and Southland and the Adam Hamilton Fund in August 1994, with no levy for parishes. The role was to be reviewed in December 1994; however Rev Townsend had already resigned in September 1994.

Parish mergers

By 1996, numerous reports express concern about the future of Southland Presbytery. Some parishes with ministers, such as Otautau/Waiono Union, were saying they could no longer afford to support their ministry due to falling membership numbers which had resulted in diminished income.

Because many parishes had employed lay pastors on short-term contracts and eight parishes had been identified as suffering hardship, Limestone Parish requested that a forum be held, not just for Western Southland parishes, but for all Southland Presbytery to examine the future of the presbytery.

They also requested that a letter be sent to all Presbyterians in Southland outlining the concerns that had been identified. They suggested a merger of several parishes with others and that no vacancies be filled until this had been achieved. An amendment to these proposals allowed parishes to fill their own vacancies, but insisted that a full review of parish boundaries, parish building requirements and future membership trends, as well as present and future requirements for ministry be carried out.

By July 1996, proposals were put forward with various options for Western valley-yoked parishes and for Central Southland to be established as clusters of parishes.

In February 1996, a report from the Futures Work Group urged parishes and the presbytery to realise that, "they should no longer expect society to follow the Gospel and come to church," but that they should feel empowered to undertake a mission approach. They should avoid a maintenance model, but rather should re-program for mission and realise that it would take time to restructure.

Some ideas which had been suggested for re-structuring of parishes and their neighbours were most enthusiastically received by the Central Southland parishes. At meetings held on 4-5 December 1996, 4-10 February 1997 (convened by Allan Paulin, Synod Secretary), parishes of Western and Central Southland discussed their various needs and possible ways of having them met, alongside options for amalgamation and co-operation between parishes.

Parishes of Eastern and Southern Southland also looked at their options and possibilities for the future. One positive outcome of these discussions was a first step towards the amalgamation of the Merrivale/ Waiau and Tuatapere/Orepuki parishes as of 21 February 1997. From March 1997 they became known as the Waiau Valley Parish, with a Service of Inauguration held on 29 June 1997 at Orawia Church.

In 1999 Otautau/Waiono Union Parish employed part-time Lay Supply ministers, Mrs Judith Day until May 2002, and Stephen and Shona Hurd from August 2002 to January 2004, as well as Summer Supply ministers. Limestone Plains undertook to have worship held in three locations on a rotational basis to replace the need for a service in each of their three locations every week.

By May 1997, a plan emerged to establish a circuit amongst the parishes of Western Southland to be facilitated by both Lay and Ordained Ministry which would provide support and leadership with due consideration for each parish's needs and keeping in mind the risk of rushing into something without an agreed process. The new ministry model, to be called the Longwood Circuit, would recognise the various services that could be provided by the Ministers involved.

By this time, the parishes of Wallacetown and St. Stephens had met and decided not to link together, and each then sought to fill their vacancies.

A comprehensive report from the Futures Committee to the Southland Presbytery dated 30 June 1997 outlines the task of the committee, the meetings held, the proposals and outcomes. It was "generally agreed that the present situation is not tenable," and eight themes were identified as follows:

a. Clergy and lay people working together in leadership

b. A mission focus rather than a chaplaincy model of ministry

c. A desire to be active in and relevant to the local community

d. Work to meet the needs of people under forty

e. A range of worship styles, with all including some contemporary music

f. The congregation as the key missional unit but several are likely to be grouped for administrative purposes and served by a ministry team of lay and ordained people, some paid full time, some part time and some voluntary

g. Minister's leadership seen as enablers and co-ordinators, sharing in innovation, rather than figureheads

h. Denominational linkage is less important than congregational home.

The report also expressed a considerable degree of frustration, mainly because congregations were little inclined or committed to such bold future options; they preferred only to put in place cosmetic changes. The report commented: "If this conservatism remains, the few options available will reduce to none at all."

Each of the regions were given a programme of steps towards progress to implement and each one concluded: "We have been in these discussions many times before. DO IT NOW!" Presbytery was strongly advised to act as the situation had reached a critical stage. At the same time, the following report was tabled from the Ministry Committee's discussion of issues relating to ministry and restructuring in the Southland Presbytery.

It covered the following topics:

1. The roots of the PCANZ as a reformed Church

2. The PCANZ's philosophy of Ministry

3. The Presbyterian Form of Church Government, as it Relates to the Ordained Ministry

4. Some Issues Affecting the Church/Presbytery at this Time:

    - The Decline of Denominationalism and the Coming Revival
    - The Problems of the PCANZ
    - What Value is the Ordained Minister?
    - The Right to Call
    - The Role of Interim Moderators, when it is no longer an Interim?

5. Recommendation for a Federal Model of Ministry

    - What it means to by a 'Federal' Model of Ministry?
    - Why is this model being proposed?
    - How should we go about implementing such a change?

6. Minister at Large in the Presbytery.

This was followed in September 1997 by the Ministry Committee's Special Report which explored the following topics:

1. "How do the proposals in the futures report fit in with the proposed federal model in the ministry committee report, with a better definition of the term 'Federal' and what groupings of parishes do we envisage?

2. How will a Federal Model provide a fairer distribution of lay and ordained Ministry Resources across the presbytery and how will it enable presbytery to better fulfil its responsibility to provide ministry to every part of the presbytery?

3. Giving further consideration to the implementation of such a proposal; a further look at the audit and how will these proposals further a Mission Focus?"

This report recommended the implementation of a complete re-structuring of all parishes into viable and appropriate groupings, to be phased in one group at a time, with presbytery employing a suitable person for three years full-time, possibly funded by the Synod of Otago and Southland Mission and Evangelism Fund and PSDS (Presbyterian Savings and Development) to oversee the work. Southland Presbytery adopted these recommendations on 2 September 1997. A job described as Oversight of Rearrangement of

Parishes in Southland Presbytery was presented in December 1997, along with terms as a part-time or full-time position. The position was advertised but remained vacant.

By June 1998, it became clear that nothing would happen if Presbytery continued to wait for the right person to apply. The convenor of the sub-committee commented that the current parish system was unworkable and that a cluster system would be better. He pointed out that there were three alternatives to achieve change, the:

a. worst method, to do it ourselves and take many years

b. best method, to do it ourselves soon with a minimum of fuss, and

c. realistic way, to employ someone to do the task.

A "Report on Progress on Future in West of the Presbytery" received by Southland Presbytery from Rev Neil Cowie, Presbytery Facilitator, in December 1998, asked: "What is going to happen in the Parishes of Limestone Plains, Riverton, Otautau/Waiono Union and Waiau Valley? Only God knows and the leaders are trying to discern His plans."

It listed the meetings that had been held and the discussions that had taken place and made the general assessment that, "each parish has got over the emotional turmoil of instability and uncertainty of the past, to become now more practical and focussed on mission."

At a meeting held on 8 November 1998, presbytery decided to consider a Longwood Parish to embrace all four parishes, with each parish appointing two "committee" representatives to meet in 1999 to consider proposals on working together and produce a "Longwood Newsletter" to communicate between parishes. This was followed by a meeting on 3 April 1999.

During this period the following parishes were vacant and looking for ministry alternatives to calling a full-time Ordained Minister.

At the time they were using various forms of leadership as follows:

- Mossburn – part-time lay supply
- Otautau/Waiono Union – part-time Methodist lay supply, Presbyterian pulpit supply Summer Supply by theology students; some Ordained Ministry supply at Ohai/Nightcaps
- Waiau Valley – part-time lay supply
- Riverton Union – Methodist Minister
- Limestone Plains – part-time Local Limited Minister
- Wallacetown – vacant, lay leadership, seeking Ordained Minister, filled January 1999
- St. Stephen's – vacant, then full-time Ordained Minister, December 1998
- St. Paul's – part-time lay supply
- Bluff Co-operating – Methodist ministry supply with lay (and some ordained) pulpit supply
- Oban – Pulpit Supply, lay and ordained (ecumenical).

Woodlands and Oteramika/Kennington also indicated they could no longer sustain full-time ordained ministry and some others, St. Paul's, Knox and St. Andrew's, indicated that the same situation was rapidly approaching for them as well.

As only 10 of the 27 parishes in the presbytery had full-time ministry, a 'Think Tank' meeting in March 2001, discussed, the abolition of parish boundaries, a focus on healthy congregations and co-operative sharing of resources. The plan was, "to develop and enter into a process of motivating congregations to develop and strengthen mission opportunities by sharing resources with other congregations who going in the same direction."

This was followed in September 2001, by a discussion paper from Allan Paulin, Co-Director of the Southern South Island Mission Resource Team, which contended that Southland Presbytery needed to make some difficult strategic decisions. He identified Invercargill and its surrounds as having 16 parishes, a much larger number than seemed necessary, and he suggested that 8 parishes would be a much more workable number. He also pointed out that, of the 27 parishes in the presbytery, only one parish had lived within its non-capital income in the last financial year.

He went on to suggest some potentially workable amalgamations and groupings (similar to the grouping or federal model previously suggested for rural parishes) of city congregations, into regional clusters, North city, Central city, and South city, with reference to some of the possible links with rural parishes close to the city. He urged the presbytery, "to act NOW as the potential to fill vacancies is limited and parishes may fall over with consequent frustration, hurt and loss."

The Report of the Joint Regional Committee (JRC) of the Uniting Congregations of Aotearoa New Zealand (UCANZ) for October 2002 noted that, in three of the western parishes (Riverton, Limestone Plains and Otautau/Waiono), there were ongoing discussions regarding co-operation between them, including sharing of ministry resources and collaboration on training for lay leaders.

A meeting held 2 December 2003 between the Mission Committee and Rev John Daniel, Synod Mission Advisor, discussed models of church for those parishes unable to sustain an ordained ministry. These models included:

1. House Church for small numbers supported by a mentor and resource minister

2. Local Ministry Teams (LMT) where there were people able to take on various roles supported by a Resource Minister, or

3. A combination of both, with a Resource Minister working with a number of parishes who could be assisted by the Mission Resource Committee of Synod to undertake a strategic review of what resourcing each parish would require for their mission and future plans.

Chapter 4 – A Presbytery In Crisis

In July 2004, Rev Dr Simon Rae, Southland Presbytery Moderator, presented a report to Presbytery entitled, "An Uncalled-for Report from the Moderator." In it, he stated that the Presbytery was in a near-terminal crisis, or 'melt-down.'

He went on to say that the presbytery was unable to function as it should, to sustain the values Assembly had identified, of safe ministry, healthy congregations and mission orientation (as opposed to survival strategies). He pointed out that the workloads of Ministers, Presbytery Elders and Presbytery Committees were too heavy, with multiple responsibilities for many people.

He highlighted a radical unwillingness to change, risk co-operation or share power, especially with reference to the Allan Paulin plan, which had been ignored, allowing parishes to just do their own thing without stable ordained ministry and a lack of personnel for Visitations and Boards of Nomination. He pointed out that ignoring Risk Management Processes could lead to abuse (and litigation) as statutory requirements for a duty of care were being neglected.

This was evident in the making of inappropriate appointments and the lack of provision for supervision. He called for parishes to be linked in Mission Units which would call a full-time Nationally Ordained Minister (NOM) for each unit. There should be one Parish Council for each unit, which would develop a mission strategy plan that would use their shared resources.

This proposal would see parishes move away from historic territorial boundaries towards dynamic, viable, community-facing mission units with strong lay leadership and stable ordained ministry. This would allow parishes to get to know each other, to act immediately to resolve issues and to sustain appropriate staffing levels. The suggestions he made about which parish would be in which unit were similar to the plan proposed by Allan Paulin.

In November 2004, parishes reported to the Mission and Ministry Committee on the proposed clustering of all parishes of Presbytery, to be identified as Central Southland Parish, Aparima Cluster, Waiau Valley Parish, Te Anau Parish, South City Cluster, Central City Cluster, North City/Rural Cluster and Eastern City/Rural Cluster.

Some of the concerns expressed were: having to attend more meetings, the need for evangelical outreach, and ministry appointment processes. Presbytery voted to hold its meetings bi-monthly (March, May, July, September and November) with the clusters meeting on the other months of the year (February, April, June, August, October and December). Each of the seven mostly regional clusters (with Te Anau to stand alone or opt in when able) would meet early in 2005 to appoint a facilitator to organise meetings.

This new arrangement would relieve the workload of Interim Moderators, some of whom were working with up to four parishes. They would then be supported by other ministers in each cluster, as there was to be at least one Ordained Minister in each cluster. This model also allowed for the inclusion of parishes in Co-operative Ventures.

However, the model did not address the distances to be travelled by some parishes, such as Mossburn, Waiau Valley and Oban, whose leaders expressed their unwillingness to attend most of the meetings. However, it was generally felt that this model of strategic planning would be a positive step towards a healthy presbytery, as proposed by the Reform Group of Assembly in its paper on Healthy Congregations.

Chapter 5 – Local Ministry Teams and the Southland Regional Resource Ministry

Terms of appointment for the setting up of Local Ministry Teams had been adopted by Assembly, which Knox Parish then undertook to achieve. However, this model also included the requirement to have a Resource Minister for each team, putting further pressure on the limited number of ministers available. Therefore, at the February 2005 meeting of the Mission and Ministry Committee, ways of providing resource ministry were suggested:

1. A NOM to be provided with 15% of stipend for working with one LMT

2. Presbytery to appoint a Resource Minister for up to five LMTs with each providing 20% of stipend

3. Presbytery to appoint a Resource Minister to coach and mentor LMTs (like a rural chaplain)

4. Suitable retired ministers to be considered as Resource Ministers for LMTs

5. A NOM within the LMT's parishes cluster to be contracted for a percentage of stipend for the role of Resource Minister within the cluster.

At this meeting the role of a Parish Enabler was also developed. It was proposed that a person might work across 4-5 parishes with each providing a percentage of their stipend. In July 2005, St. Paul's Parish also indicated their intention to form a Local Ministry Team.

Another strategy adopted by the presbytery to reduce the workload for Interim Moderators, was to appoint an Elder to moderate Session meetings to save the moderator from having to moderate every meeting. Traditionally Interim Moderators, while being Minister in another parish, also chaired Session and Congregational Meetings, conducted weddings, funerals and sacraments, in the absence of ordained clergy in the vacant parish they were Interim Moderator for.

The new role of Moderating Elder was instigated on the understanding that the Moderating Elder would seek advice and guidance from NOM's when needed and make it known to whom parishioners could approach in matters of complaint. This role was then adopted by Oban, Limestone Plains, Mossburn, Wallacetown and St Stephen's as well as Woodlands, Oteramika/Kennington, PIC (Pacific Island Church), Richmond Grove and Toitois. The committee also made allowance for the short-term appointment of lay ministers (six months at a time) to alleviate the lack of LOMs and NOMs, especially in the situation where there was not an Ordained Minister in each of the cluster groups.

This dearth of clergy was also making it difficult to find appropriate resource Ministers for LMTs. It was also indicated that some members of LMTs might benefit from attending courses provided by Knox School of Ministry, and that if they did so this would be recognised as Continuing Ministry formation. Alongside these proposals the need was also highlighted for elders to be trained and commissioned to conduct baptisms, and the Sacrament of Holy Communion.

Following on from the Synod Review of Presbyteries in April 2006, the Mission and Ministry Committee prepared a report on the Revised Functions of Congregational Clusters, and the Cluster make-up was revised as well. Key roles of the cluster group were defined, and the parishes in each cluster were identified along with key personnel in each cluster.

I was personally involved as the APW (Association of Presbyterian Women) representative to Presbytery, beginning in February 2003, then later as a member of the Presbytery Executive and convenor of the Administration Committee. I can recall that with regard to the cluster groupings of parishes, the bi-monthly meetings became more and more difficult to plan, with fewer and fewer representatives attending. Within a year or so, support for this model diminished to the point that it was no longer tenable, with communication between parishes cited as one of the difficulties. This then left a significant vacuum of ministry oversight for a significant number of vacant parishes. Ten parishes in the Presbytery were identified as having an Interim Moderator; three had established Local Ministry Teams over the years since 2005, two had a Resource Minister and was one still looking for a RM, and two had Lay Supply ministers. Interim Moderators were responsible for three parishes. One parish, was a Co-operating Venture under Presbyterian oversight. Four parishes were identified as remote and unable to be linked with or supported by a neighbouring parish.

The first Local Ministry Team at Knox Presbyterian Church in Invercargill was closely followed by the commissioning of a Local Ministry Team at St Paul's, Invercargill, and then St Stephen's. In December 2007, 12 parishes in the previous Southland Presbytery that were classed as being vacant and being led by lay members, with oversight by Interim Moderators. This situation had come about during the preceding ten years, when congregation numbers were in decline, and finances were insufficient to employ an Ordained Minister.

Four streams of ministry have been identified by the Presbyterian Church of Aotearoa New Zealand,

- Nationally Ordained Minister (NOM)
- Locally Ordained Ministry (LOM)
- Local Ministry Team (LMT) and
- Amorangi (or Māori Minister)

These roles were being developed at this time.

The third stream was the preferred option for many parishes, who then commissioned a team of lay leaders as an LMT to take responsibility for key roles in the church, such as worship leader, mission leader, pastoral care leader, and sometimes other roles such as administrator or pastor.

While the requirement for these lay teams is to have a Resource Minister, it was recognised that there were very few Ordained Ministers available in Southland, or willing to move to Southland, who could undertake this role. A small group of presbytery members met to write a job description and set up a Ministry Settlement Board, convened by Rev Ian Crawford. The role was initially described as a Presbytery Ministry Enabler, who would work half time for St Paul's Church and half time for five other parishes – Wallacetown, Knox, Otautau/Waiono, St Stephen's and Limestone Plains.

A meeting was held at St Paul's Church on 9 August 2008 to discuss issues relating to ministry, support for parishes with LMTs, Pastoral Assistants or Lay Assistants, at which the need for Resource Ministry was confirmed. The position was advertised in national publications, and on the SPANZ and PCANZ websites, but there were no applicants. This was not surprising as very few would have a concept of what the role would entail. The Ministry Settlement Board reported in July 2009 that 17 people had been approached.

As it became clear that someone was needed to undertake this role sooner rather than later, it was thought that someone already resident in Southland might be able to take on the role. At the time, as a Locally Ordained Minister (LOM), Rev Heather Kennedy could change her employment status, no longer providing Ministry Supply for ten hours a week at Bluff/Greenhills Co-operating Parish, along with 30 hours a week at First Church. Rev Ian Crawford, (also a LOM, previously a Baptist Pastor), was in a similar position, ending a five-year ministry at St David's Parish, with some oversight of St Paul's.

Together they made a proposal and were interviewed by the Ministry Settlement Board on 29 October 2009. Presbytery decided that they could take on the role, jointly, of Resource Ministers for Southland parishes that did not have a minister, myself for 20 hours a week (and 20 hours at First Church) and Rev Ian Crawford for 10 hours a week (and 30 hours Ministry Supply at Windsor Community Church). This also enabled all those Ministers in Southland who were Interim Moderators of those parishes not seeking to fill their vacancy, to be discharged of this responsibility.

Each parish without an Ordained Minister was invited to commit to this initiative and a rationale of levied contribution towards the funding was calculated. An application to the Synod of Otago and Southland to gain major funding for three years of the project was sent, and the outcome was affirmative.

After a meeting with parish representatives in November 2009, nine of twelve possible parishes committed to the partnership proposal and, after two more meetings, agreed to proceed with Rev Ian Crawford supplying quarter time and Rev Heather Kennedy half time for a period of three years, with annual reviews.

They were duly inducted at a service on 2 February 2010, at St Paul's Presbyterian Church, Invercargill, for a three-year term.

The member parishes of the Southland Regional Resource Ministry were Oban (Stewart Island), Bluff Greenhills Co-operating, St Paul's, St Stephen's, Wallacetown, Limestone Plains, Otautau-Waiono, Waiau Valley and Mossburn. They ranged from Tuatapere in the West to Mossburn in the North of Southland, to Bluff, south of Invercargill and Stewart Island. The furthest distance from Invercargill is to Mossburn, 100kms, with Tuatapere almost as far, and to get to Stewart Island it is necessary to cross Foveaux Strait by air or ferry. St Paul's and St Stephen's are city parishes, and Wallacetown is nearby.

Those parishes opting out were Knox, Oteramika-Kennington and Woodlands. However, if their arrangements had been unsustainable due to a lack of Ordained Ministers to be Interim Moderators or Resource Ministers, they may well have looked at their options for the future and considered joining the Regional Resource Ministry at a later date.

In addition to the parishes mentioned, the parishes of First Church, Windsor Community, St. Andrew's and St. David's in Invercargill, Central Southland and Te Anau were able to support full time ministry, and Richmond Grove had a part-time minister, while Riverton and Otatara, as CVs (Co-operating Ventures) were under Methodist oversight.

When Rev Ian Crawford and Rev Heather Kennedy were commissioned to this new role, there was no job description and no outline of expectations, as they were yet to be written. Parishes were asked what they thought the role should entail and what their specific ministry needs were. Some of the roles that were identified were:

- taking services of worship, as and when able, on pulpit supply rosters
- pastoral care, supervision and support of Local Ministry Team members and
- members of Parish Council-led parishes

- providing training for team members, especially for Licensed Communion and Baptism Elders and for those with specific responsibilities, such as pastoral visitors, and
- providing resources, educational opportunities and networking.

During 2011, Rev Kennedy took Study Leave to attend a course in the UK on 'Multi-Parish Ministry' and visited many areas where similar ministries were being provided in England, Wales and Scotland.

The ministry role was assessed informally after one year, at the first Annual Meeting of the Regional Resource Ministry, where it was endorsed, with encouragement to continue providing ministry to those parishes involved.

Rev Crawford and Rev Kennedy continued to provide leadership for the member parishes as Resource Ministers for the contracted three years. A review process was then instigated by Southern Presbytery, since Southland Presbytery had ceased to exist and was by then part of the much larger Presbytery which covers the same geographical region as the Synod of Otago and Southland.

Rev Crawford had committed one week each month of the year to make himself available to an assigned parish on a rostered basis by leading worship on Sunday and providing any resources that parish currently needed.

On the other hand, Rev Kennedy responded to invitations by member parishes to fill the pulpit when requested, undertook the provision of funeral services, attended Parish Council meetings on a regular basis and provided resource input for specific situations.

Both Resource Ministers worked together in providing resource workshops on sacraments, pastoral care, as well as liturgy and lectionary. However, these were not always well attended.

Chapter 6 – A Proposal to Reform Presbyteries

The following is a questionnaire circulated by the Presbytery Reform Group of Assembly which helped facilitate the process put to the General Assembly in 2008. The answers were provided by members of the Commission of Southland Presbytery, made up of the Moderator, Clerk and Chairs of the Governance and Resource Committees.

What changes has your Presbytery made over the last two to three years in the way you operate as a Presbytery, and what positive effect have you discerned from these changes?

It has changed from a purely business model to one where the bulk of the business is done by a Commission of Presbytery. Presbytery meets once every three months for business and in the intervening months, as clusters (groups of parishes based mainly on geographical location) and as a resource meeting.

Many feel the work of presbytery is remote, and when we do gather to discuss business, it is only the business relevant to that time, many decisions have been made between these meetings by the Commission.

In seeking to fulfill your obligations as a Presbytery name the biggest challenge you currently face?

Under the present system, comments have been made about the difficulty of actually getting to know people and connecting with them in any meaningful way. The lack of Nationally Ordained Minister's (NOM) of Word and Sacrament with a broad knowledge and working life in the wider church is a challenge to this Presbytery.

What features of Presbytery life are most valued, and need to be preserved whatever the future may be?

Presbytery must continue to act and fulfill its role as a court of the church with its function of oversight of parishes, ensuring that proper process and accountability is maintained. We seem to be slipping further and further into a model of congregationalism, which for many good reasons Presbyterianism has sought to refrain from.

Presbytery has primarily a business function, not a mission one. Its attempts to ensure that mission happens in the local parish have not been well supported. Presbytery does not need to have a vital and enthusiastic life of its own, but rather must work to ensure that Parishes do. Sometimes people expect too much of the wrong thing from presbytery.

The following questionnaire was circulated to all parishes for their response. The response from First Presbyterian Church, Invercargill is given as a typical example from one of the few parishes which replied.

Questions & Responses for Parishes in the Southland Presbytery

How do you feel about the current plan of meetings for Southland Presbytery?

If this is the pattern and way in which presbytery is to continue then the pattern is fine, however as you will see from the other questions at First Church, we have some misgivings about the new mode of operation of presbytery.

Is this system working effectively? What are the strengths and weaknesses of this system?

We do not believe it is working effectively, depending on what is meant by that word. If business is getting done, probably, but it is being done by a small, probably overworked group of people, and the regular members of presbytery, (those nominated by their parishes) are being left with very little if any part in a lot of the decision process and even less in the discussions behind any decisions.

Are you happy with the way the Commission functions? What do you see as the strengths and weaknesses?

They do the job that is required of them, and probably do it well, but the principle is one we are not happy with, as alluded to previously. The members of the commission seem to be exclusive and there is not enough discussion. The majority of members of presbytery are disempowered and that means not every parish is involved in some quite important decisions that are being made.

What topics would you like presented at Resource Meeting?

As you can see we would rather have presbytery meetings that deal with business and if there is an occasion where a particular issue needs fuller discussion then have that as the main focus of the presbytery meeting, or hold a workshop at another time.

How effective is your Cluster? Does it need changes?

It is very hard to get people interested. We meet only to dream up ways to do things together and only a very, very small number of people attend. Parishes within the cluster share very little in common, more beneficial links could be made with other parishes.

It is hard to justify putting parishes' time and energy into these cluster meetings when there is virtually no support or desire to support them from the pews.

Overall, it might be better if presbytery worked on a bi-monthly meeting where we conduct the usual business of presbytery, and view that as our function and role, rather than trying to create a body that has a life of its own sapping the precious resources from our parishes that should be spending that energy on their mission in the local community.

At General Assembly held in 2008, it was proposed: that the General Assembly adopt the model for the Reform of Presbyteries with each presbytery establishing a Presbytery Reform Team with appropriately skilled missional leaders to implement the model. The Team would consult with other Presbyteries and Union District Councils to establish a reconfiguration of presbytery boundaries, establish Resourcing Groups and establish new governance structures.

It was also proposed that: the Presbytery Reform Team would be established by the beginning of 2009, that Presbyteries begin operating within the new Presbytery Structure by October 2009, with the implementation of the new model, and that the new presbyteries begin operating within the new Presbytery Structure as soon as is practicable and that the new presbytery boundaries be formalised by the General Assembly. Council of Assembly would oversee the implementation of tasks vested in national bodies. The Presbyteries Task Group would co-ordinate presbyteries and their Presbytery Reform Teams in the implementation of the model and monitor progress and report to the 2010 General Assembly.

General Assembly adopted the model for the Reform of Presbyteries as outlined. The motion was agreed to.

Therefore, in order to prepare for this transition, a Combined Presbytery Reform Team was formed in 2009 with two representatives from each Presbytery, being Dunedin and North Otago, South Otago, Central Otago, Mataura and Southland. Rev Heather Kennedy (replacing Rev Karl Lamb) and Zona Pearce, represented Southland Presbytery and continued in that role on the Presbytery Council of the Southern Presbytery, when it was inaugurated in February 2010 (with Zona Pearce taking on the role of Presbytery Clerk).

In 2009 Southland Presbytery amalgamated all its committees' roles into the Governance Team and the Resource Workgroup, and changed its meetings to once every two months, without the formatted meeting structure. Members met for a short worship component and a meal provided by the host parish, followed by a short report from the Administration Committee, with any business that needed ratification. Then a resource component followed as organised by the Resource Workgroup, which in November 2010 became known as EquipSouth.

The Southern Presbytery was Inaugurated at Calvin Church in Gore, on Saturday 13 February 2010.

A Worship Service for the Closing of the Southland Presbytery was conducted by the last Moderator of Presbytery, Rev Richard Gray, in the Central Southland Parish church in Winton on Tuesday 2 November 2010, at the first meeting of EquipSouth.

So, in 2010, after 145 years from its establishment the Presbytery of Southland, comprised of 22 Charges, was incorporated into the Southern Presbytery, which includes all Charges south of the Waitaki

River – the territorial extent of the Synod of Otago and Southland. The Presbytery of Southland having come full circle in its links with all the other congregations and Presbyteries of the south.

Chapter 7 – Notes from the minutes

1990

- Workshop in March on 'Releasing the Church into the Ministry of Healing' with Delores Winder, Inc. Creative Healing, Prayer Life, Spiritual Growth, Church Planning, Worship and Healing
- April, celebration on 125th year of Presbytery
- Catherine Hollister-Jones visits in June, presents concept of Prayer Triangles
- Looking at parish boundaries, Futures Committee looking at possibilities for models of ministry
- 'Ministry with Children and Adults' Training Weekend on 'Sharing Faith with Children' pack
- In August a 'Church History Seminar' with Margaret Morgan and Rev John McKean
- Permission granted for the training of Elders to administer the sacraments
- 'Parish Futures Commission' attended October Presbytery meeting
- One Quinquennial visitation and one camp visitation recorded in the year

1991

- Waiau Valley parishes linked
- March, Southland Youth Trust requiring funding for Youth Director's role of empowering Youth Leaders and parishes
- Graham Miller, PCANZ Education and Lay Ministry Advisor visits Western parishes
- Easter Camps held at Edenview and Riverton for different age groups
- June, Presbytery Prayer Retreat at Pounawea, Riverton
- Port Visits in Bluff and Oban, 8 September, for 50th Anniversary of the Navy, worship service lead by Rev David North, Naval Chaplain

- Oban applies to leave Beneficiary Fund; no minister for 50 years, but declined, resulted in being yoked to St. Andrew's. Presbytery pays arrears
- November, General Assembly held at First Church, Invercargill
- Three Quinquennial visitations and one other visitation in the year

1992

- March, Moderator toured all parishes in Presbytery
- Studied 'Church Futures' document
- Discussed use of titles and honorifics ('Pastor' not a Presbyterian title for minister), standing for the Moderator and recognition of roles
- 'Children in Church' seminar lead by Rev Sherri Weinberg, at Winton
- Presbytery Elders urged to report back to Parish Councils, including reports from Synod
- Flood Emergency Fund established in 1984 to be dispersed as no longer required
- Spiritual Growth seminars held with Rev Jim Young
- Reminder regarding confidentiality of information regarding patients in hospital
- October, 'Heartwood' project launched, for parishes – from 'Maintenance to Mission' focussing on Christian Education, Lay Ministry, Clergy Support and Continued Education for Clergy
- Futures Committee looks at the viability of parishes with possible boundary changes, to work with each other, support small parishes, share resources, look for possibilities and opportunities, celebrate successes and utilise programs
- Synod Youth Roadshow, in November, focussing on Tuatapere and Otautau and training Youth Leaders
- December, guidelines for Sacramental Elders discussed.
- Synod guidelines on dispersal of property outlined
- Five Quinquennial visitations completed in 1992

1993

- Presbytery Retreat held at Camp Taringatura in March. Poorly attended by city parishes. Focused on: relationship, communication, trust in God, mutual support and innovation
- Voting on remit being sent to Assembly on the Ordination and Induction of Self-Avowed Active Homosexuals. Remit not passed at Assembly. No ordinations or inductions of homosexuals until Special Assembly Committee reports
- Overture to Assembly on the shortening of Ordination training by one year in recognition of prior learning/qualifications
- Overture to Assembly on allowing full-time Lay Ministers full membership of Presbytery
- Presbyterian Support Chaplains in rest homes not to be considered a replacement for parish ministers, who should continue visiting parishioners
- Presbytery Retreat, in July on 'Moving in Mission' and Growth Evangelism
- Followed later in the year by Lay Preachers Course for seven participants, 'Gossiping the Gospel' at First Church, well received by 47 attendees
- Mission Statement for Southland Presbytery formulated[1]
- Monthly prayer breakfasts held at First Church, sometimes elsewhere
- August; parishes identified as 'not seeking to fill vacancies' are Mossburn/Te Anau, Oban and Woodlands, have Interim Moderators appointed
- Ministers may not use 'liberty of conscience' with regard to baptism of infants and believers
- All ministers (and wives) to have Supervision

---

1. The Mission of the Presbytery of Southland is to Advance the Kingdom of God by:
   - Representing Christ to the Community
   - Effective Oversight of Ministers and Parishes
   - Resourcing and Enabling people and parishes
   - Linking with General Assembly and the Wider Church Under the Leadership of God's Spirit.

- Ministers to undertake 70 hours per year of Development Training/ Study, especially on units in the Book of Order on: Preparing Couples for Marriage and the Marriage service, Funeral services and related matters, Children in Worship/Children's talks, and Supervision
- September: Recommendation that parishes preparing for Quinquennial Visitations have a training session
- In October: Disappointment expressed by rural parishes regarding training workshops scheduled during Spring
- Property Committee calling for women members to provide balance
- Six Quinquennial visitations undertaken

1994

- February, a register of Ministry Formation is established to record hours completed by Ministers
- Otatara United Church becomes Otatara Community Church
- 'Job Descriptions' formulated for all Presbytery Committees
- A Regional Advisor for Otago and Southland is appointed by Assembly to troubleshoot situations early and give advice
- A review of Youth Ministry undertaken to define lines of accountability in relationship with parish groups, Youth director, SPY Executive, Presbytery Mission Committee, Christian Youth Trust and Presbytery. A convoluted structure which needed clarification
- SPY constitution re-write and lines of accountability defined
- Presbytery Reform response – more lay representation deemed unwieldy, gender balance achievable, no age limit preferring people with faith, ability and experience, need to moderate debate, deliberation and discussion, non-members with skills to be sought for committee
- Parish Mission Consultant recommends creation of a 'think tank' to identify Presbytery's most urgent needs
- A Special Meeting of Presbytery was held in November, to look at Youth Ministry, especially the role and funding for the Youth Director
- After many years of Presbytery meeting at First Church it was decided in November that parishes could offer to host and cater for

the monthly meetings, with suggestions to car-pool to avoid large mileage claims from city ministers attending rural meetings

- December, Lay Preachers training in lectionary, liturgy, prayer, preparation and resources for children's talks
- First thoughts for a Tertiary Chaplaincy at Southern Institute of Technology
- Contact persons appointed for complaints of sexual misconduct
- Youth Directorate re-starts from 'level playing field'
- Four Quinquennial visits completed, with re-defined process outlines

1995

- February meeting held at Peacehaven Chapel, reminder to have reports in on time and to be concise
- Presbytery Retreat to encourage Mission Statement, sharing resources and ideas.
- Heartwood project re-named Discovery, a way to formulate Mission Statements
- Pacific Island Church (PIC) Youth visit Auckland and Wellington to experience different worship styles, cultures and ways of fund-raising
- SPY holds a Faith Festival at Camp Columba, Pukerau, 540 attend
- April, workload of ministers with roles on Presbytery committees highlighted
- Extra meeting held a week after the April meeting to conclude business held over
- May, Review of Presbytery undertaken – workload needs to be alleviated, retain meal for fellowship time, business and agenda to be streamlined
- Five Faces of Mission adopted by Assembly[2]

---

2. The Presbyterian Church of Aotearoa New Zealand believes it is called by God to work with others in making Jesus Christ known through:
- Teaching and nurturing people in Christian faith
- Loving service responding to human need
- Proclaiming the gospel
- Seeking to transform society
- Caring for God's creation

- Workshop held in July for Parish Treasurers
- Reminder that Hospital Visitors are not able to view patient's records, and that all Parish Rolls to be considered as private information
- After review in July it was decided to discontinue the Youth director position as a new approach is sought
- As suggested by the Public Questions committee a public profile of Presbytery is promoted, with a news sheet for parishes after each meeting, and developing a Media Policy for the Press Officer, Clerk and Moderator of Presbytery
- Sharing news from parishes at Presbytery recommended in August, to include recent events, new initiatives, unexpected outcomes; what they did, why, and the effect on the parish
- Ministers record of training reviewed. Some exceed requirements, some do very little. Currently 15 ministers on the register
- Eastern Southland parishes not wanting to merge, but to have a forum on their future, especially for Limestone Palins and Otautau/ Waiono
- Looking at Ministry models beyond 2000
- In response to Homosexuality and the Church debate, Southland Presbytery declares it will not licence gay ministers
- Four Quinquennial visits, including Camp Taringatura and one Special Commission to North parish

1996

- Training day at Taringatura
- Rev Kimi Henry ordained as LLM – Local Limited Supply for PIC in February, also for Māori from July
- 76 attend Presbytery Retreat
- 460 attend Faith Festival at Cromwell
- New possibilities for a new structure for Presbytery, research to be undertaken
- Review undertaken of Presbytery Clerk position
- Survival Training held in May for those who were attending Assembly

- Eleven parishes vacant, urgent need for Interim Moderators and members of Boards of Nomination; possible amalgamations suggested
- 80 attended Easter Camp at Tautuku
- InterChurch Trade and Industry Chaplaincy changes name to Workplace Chaplaincy
- Working Committee set up for property projects scheduled for 1998-2002
- Parishes to compile Asset Registers for insurance purposes; recommendation to rationalise land and building ownership
- Council of Assembly proposes Biennial Assemblies
- September, note made that Moderator of Presbytery be involved in APW Presbyterial meetings, especially Communion services and AGM
- Role descriptions for Presbytery Committees to be re-visited
- Review of Youth Directors and Christian Youth Trust's roles needed
- Large funding needed to revamp Camp Taringatura, viability to be investigated

1997

- Rock's Church, Riverton, closed, articles from Rock's and Groper's Bush given to Riverton parish, buildings to be sold
- 'Habitat for Humanity' premises opens in Glengarry
- Māori Chaplain joins Hospital Chaplaincy team
- Centre Bush and Oteramika Kennington parishes declared vacant, no longer able to support ministry, as with many other parishes identified as small uneconomic units
- Planning for a Central Southland Parish commences, to combine Oreti, Centre Bush, Forest Hill and Winton (and Dipton)
- All parishes are urged to pay the recommended Lay and Ordained ministers supply fee. All levies to be paid to Assembly Office
- Proceeds from sale of property only to be used for property purchase or maintenance, but not to pay stipends
- No Assembly this year, to become Biennial, with some annual arrangements to be changed to suit

- Waiau Valley parish inaugurated in June, combined parishes of Orawia and Tuatapere
- Mossburn and Te Anau parishes separate
- Cook Is. Parish closes Bluff (Ocean Beach) church and move back to Ness Street PIC
- Te Anau parish becomes Lakeside Church
- Financial implications of having a Presbytery 'Minister at Large' considered
- Presbytery votes 29 to 10 in favour of supporting the Assembly decision to ban ordination of homosexuals. Parishes vote 19 to 8 in favour
- Role description drawn up for person to Oversee a Rearrangement of Parishes in the Presbytery
- One Quinquennial visitation and one formal visitation undertaken

1998

- Need to catch up on visitations signalled
- Church Life Survey to be used to audit Presbytery parishes. Seven indicators[3] were used to assess health of the parish
- Brown's church bell restored and installed at Hedgehope. Forest Hills church sold
- Hawthorndale church closed in March
- Preparation of a Contract to be used when making Lay Appointments
- Camp Taringatura looking at options for land use; to be developed by Department of Conservation? Planted as forest? Or sold? Decide to keep their 'rough it' style
- Ministerial Evaluation recorded. 29 ministry positions: 14 filled by Ordained Ministers, 8 Lay Ministers, seven vacant. Only three Ordained Minsters outside of Invercargill city
- Rationalisation of city parishes recommended due to population decline
- Recommended that parishes considering amalgamation be excused from quinquennial visitation

---

3. Outward focus • Level of involvement • Sense of community • Direction or purpose • Inspiring leadership • People of lively faith • Newcomers attracted

- Resistance to reshaping Presbytery due: fear of change, fear of loss of identity, misunderstanding of process, confusion about structures and particularity of mindsets.
- Hawthorndale, Orawia and Orepuki church buildings sold
- Four Quinquennial Visitations and two special visits.

1999

- Extra Assembly on Unity and Diversity held in February in Christchurch
- Central Southland Parish Council established
- Cook Island parish based at St Andrew's after splitting from Pacific Island Church (Samoan)
- Waianawa Church deconsecrated in July
- Orepuki and Eastern Bush churches sold
- Forest Hill and Limestone Plains sell manses
- Presbyterian Hall at Bluff sold
- 'Planzwork' retreats – How to facilitate vacant parishes, help small parishes, plan for and select interim and lay ministers, focus on mission an exhibit leadership
- 'How we work as a Presbytery' Task Group reports – value relationships, meal, support and encouragement, value devotions, music, message and prayer, value efficiency and security of business procedure
- Need to review and overhaul Quinquennial Visitation Process
- Two Quinquennials and two visits in the year

2000

- Statistics for ten years 1989-1990: Communicant membership in Invercargill down by 35.5%, giving down by 29.1%, church attendance down by 43%, one new parish established, one parish self-supported without using reserves
- Presbytery review – now more caring, less judgemental and confrontational; bi-monthly meetings, to move around parishes from 5.30pm for devotions, meal and prayer; mixture of less formal input; streamlined agenda

- Interim Moderator's Vacancy Reports to be re-named Parish Ministry Report
- Ryal Bush church sold
- Presbytery Clerk review of role undertaken
- New meeting style for 2002: monthly except January at 5.30pm; alternate between 'business' and 'resource'; resource to include speakers or events open to all – to replace 'orders of the day'; improve communication Presbytery-wide; business matters by agenda
- Southland Presbyterian Youth disbanded, new direction sought for youth ministries
- Two Quinquennial Visitation and four Parish Appraisals undertaken

2001

- 50th anniversary of Richmond Grove parish
- Central Southland parish (CSPP) inaugurated in February
- Southland parishes only contributing 50% of national budget levy
- Greenhills Church building gifted to the community in March
- Historic Parish boundaries abolished, due to greater mobility of people and variety of worship styles
- Move to 'fall from' Quinquennial Visitations for 2001 and focus on building inspections and parish appraisals
- All ministers, ordained and lay strongly urged, again, to have regular Supervision
- Churches Agency on Social Issues (formerly Public Questions) recommends prompt, clear and effective advocacy on issues, which could be difficult in light of the process required to go through the appropriate church courts
- A working group established to work towards a Chaplaincy for Tertiary Education providers
- Seminar for retiring Ministers held in October
- One Parish Appraised undertaken

2002

- Lay Assistants to have speaking rights at Presbytery meetings, but not voting rights
- Presbytery Purpose Statement confirmed:
    - To stimulate and support the total mission of ministries in the Presbytery
    - To mobilise the People of God
    - To provide oversight of ministry matters, the minister's supervision scheme, minister's study leave and continuing ministry formation
    - To monitor accountability of minister, lay supply appointees and parish
    - To facilitate assessment and supervision of student or ministry
    - To consider matters relating to co-operating and union parish and ecumenical ministries
- Camp Longwood, Riverton to be sold as a going concern
- Lay appointment contracts to be examined
- Two parish visits carried out

2003

- Camp Taringatura could be sold, but 'interim committee' to manage until reassessment in 2005
- Adjustments made to the Single Assessment for parishes to assist National funding – half a percentage and half a rate per minister, assets and bequests exempt
- Discussion on merging Presbyteries in the region – a 'Big Presbytery' could cause more work and more problems
- Communion Elders to have a refresher course before being relicensed
- Browns Parish Centennial in June
- Resource meetings bi-monthly to only have short 'emergency' business beforehand

- Discussions between St. David's and Knox parishes ended – no sense of connection. Knox to consider Local Ministry Team (LMT) model, with a Resource Minister to be appointed
- Lay Appointee training in Riverton
- Co-operating Ventures becomes Uniting Congregations on Aotearoa New Zealand
- Noted that visitations are not being done
- Presbytery identifies areas such as Youth falling behind, due to lack of energy
- Need for Resource Ministers for LMT's and parishes without Ordained Ministry
- Four informal reports on parish activities received through the year

2004

- Terms of Reference for Mission and Ministry Committee defined as made up of workgroups for: Candidates for Ministry, Strategic Planning, Evangelism and Outreach, Supervision of Ministry(Including Study Leave and Christian Ministry Formation), Congregation Reviews, Training and Mission Overseas
- In light of the government closure and merger of primary schools in Invercargill, Presbytery again looks as possible parish mergers. Three options proposed:
    1. To consolidate parishes into groups of 100-200 parishioners-selling all surplus buildings
    2. To form clusters of congregations with a Nationally Ordained Minster (NOM) as oversight
    3. Locally Ordained Minster (LOM) / LMT with Resource Minister
- Follow-up on new Presbytery Meeting feedback regarding some inability to have good discussions due to differing opinions, need for more informal gatherings to share Parish news, upcoming events and celebrations
- Training for Lay Ministers in taking Funerals and Weddings
- Since the removal of parish boundaries, parishes are required to provide pastoral care over much wider areas, sometimes found to be challenging

- To enable Strategic Planning Presbytery need to set a direction that is Christ-centred, Spirit empowered and mission focussed
- First LOM in New Zealand ordained at Te Anau
- Workshop with Rev Dr John Roxburgh at Knox on 'Managing Change in the Church'
- 50th Anniversary of Waverley parish
- Cluster Plan presented to October Presbytery meeting by Mission and Ministry Committee
- Clusters to meet together in March, May, July and September in place of Presbytery meetings for those months, under the guidance of a convenor[4]
- Two Appraisals and two formal visitations

2005

- 'Possibilities for Rural Ministry' from a seminar in Adelaide presented
- LMT at Riverton
- Pastoral Safety course at North Invercargill in August
- Congregational Appraisal model to be used by Board of Nomination and Boards of Discernment in the process of forming LMT's and when referring candidates for LOM/NOM
- Not enough finances available for a Presbytery-wide Resource Minister
- Synod Review of Presbytery Report received, many familiar suggestions and some that were considered unachievable as was found difficult to find enough minsters and elders for the roles required
- PIC Cook Island amalgamate with St. Andrew's with continued services at Clarendon
- Presbytery reminded of PCANZ Employment Practices, Privacy, Health and Safety legal obligations
- LMT at St. Paul's commissioned

---

4. See Chapter 4

2006

- To alleviate yearly retraining for ministry roles a log is to be kept, to register competency in preaching, academic achievements, training courses undertaken, Communion and Baptism roles, especially for NOM's, LOM's, LMT's and Lay Supply
- Presbytery meeting schedule from April to November outlined as: Clusters, Resource, Business, Clusters, Resource, Business, Clusters, Business – mixed response to cluster meeting concept. Some co-operation, some experience difficulties
- First Church hosts 150th celebrations for Invercargill City
- 'Leadership for 20th Century' workshop held in August
- Mossburn parish 100th.
- Waverley and North Invercargill Parishes to merge at Windsor Castle Street site, Waverley site sold to Harvestfield Church. Parish to be called Windsor Community Church (Presbyterian)
- Presbytery Elders appointed to Mossburn Parish Council to assist in processes to be undertaken, due to difficulties

2007

- Presbytery Executive established, made up of Moderator, Clerk, Treasurer, Chair of Resource Committee and Chair of Business Committee, Convenor of Mission and Ministry, Property convenor and Convenor of Public Questions email group
- Mossburn Parish Council replaced by Interim Management Team
- Otatara Mission Team visits Vanuatu
- Funds held for special purposes amalgamated into general funds
- All parishes required to register with the Charities Commission. Training sessions for Treasurers held
- Joint Regional Council (JRC) to cover all of Otago and Southland
- CSPP opens new complex in Winton
- Presbyteries Task Group Report not seen as appropriate for Southland. Would prefer to work on improving current practice, to better serve parish in Southland.[5]

---

5. See Chapter 6

- St. Paul's Youth trip to Samoa
- Review of Clusters – not seen as successful, with a preference to returning to monthly Presbytery meetings. Clusters disbanded
- Flood funds, no longer required, $4000 each gifted to southland Tertiary Chaplaincy and Southland Hospital Chaplaincy

2008

- Presbytery new schedule. Business meeting monthly with fellowship meal and resource input
- Due to difficulty of providing Resource Ministers a proposal to provide a Resource Minister for all LMT's by Presbytery is to be investigated.[6] Discussions followed
- Waiau Valley parish members visit Russia on a mission venture
- Two presbytery representatives elected to work on the Presbyteries Reform Team for Otago and Southland
- Southland Christian Library set up at Richmond Grove church

2009

- In response to progress towards the Presbytery merger, all business matters of committees are amalgamated into a Governance Team; Resource Team to prepare input and programmes for Resource meetings of Presbytery
- Visit to Southland by 'Kids Friendly' Team
- Resource Team challenged to 'inspire' Presbytery
- Limestone Plains, Wallacetown, Waiau Valley parishes under the oversight of CSPP
- St. Paul's Shared Ministry model refreshed
- Otautau Sunday School Hall sold to New Life
- Presbytery Reform being managed by a Standing Committee, then becomes a merged Presbytery with an elected Presbytery Council[7]
- Plans for a Southland Presbytery Enabler proceed[8]
- Toitois parish amalgamates with St. Andrew's
- New presbytery to be called Southern Presbytery. Southland had suggested Great Southern Presbytery

6. See Chapter 5
7. See Chapter 6
8. See Chapter 5

- Final meeting of Southland Presbytery held in December
- Regional Group will meet bi-monthly

2010

- Inauguration of Southland Regional Resource Group with Induction Service at St. Paul's on 2 February. Previous Interim Moderators of parishes released from their roles
- Inauguration of Southern Presbytery held at Calvin Church in Gore on 13 February
- Southern Regional Resource Group first meeting in March – to be known as EquipSouth
- PIC Samoan to work with First Church on plans for the future. Church closed in July
- Otautau/Waiono Parish Union with Methodist Church dissolved. 12% of the value of properties to be given to Methodist Church
- All funds lodged into General Fund, $12,000 given to Southern Presbytery. $8,434.75 set aside for Southland parishes, from the Facilitator Fund
- Southland Representatives on Southern Presbytery Workgroups appointed
- SPY funds used to send a Youth Rep to GA10
- St. Paul's establishes LMT, commissioned in June
- Remaining General Funds transferred to Southland Resource Group (EquipSouth)
- Lakeside (Te Anau) Parish 50th anniversary in September
- LMT commissioned at Mossburn in October
- Church at Browns is sold
- Celebrations Service to close Southland Presbytery held at Winton on 2 November.

Presbytery Records

At the close of The Southland Presbytery all records were lodged at the Church Archives Centre, Knox College, Dunedin. These records include all minutes and committee reports, financial reports, property reports, terms of call and appointments, Public Questions topics, and correspondence inwards and outwards, as well as all notes made by myself.

Tables

Clerks of Southland Presbytery – 1990 - 2010

Name	Started	Retired
Mrs R. Adamson	June 1984	June 1990
Mrs J. Telford	June 1990	June 1995
Rev R. Townsend	June 1995	December 1995
Rev A. Matheson	January 1996	December 2004
Mrs Z. Pearce	February 2006	November 2010

Moderators of Southland Presbytery – 1990 - 2010

Started	Name	Parish
1990	Rev N.D. Cowie (to June 1990)	St. Paul's
1991	Rev James McKinlay	Knox
1992	Rev M. Lau'ese	Browns
1993	(May 1992-May 1993)	
1995	Rev N. Burns (June 1993)	St. Andrew's
1997	Rev B. Rodgers	PSS Chaplain
1997	Rev B. Doig (to July 1997)	St. David's
1998	Rev N. Jackson (August 1997)	Winton
1999	Rev B. Williscroft (August 1998)	First
2000	Rev K. Henry	PIC Cook Island /Māori
2001	Rev N. Jackson	Winton
2003	Rev D. Gordon	Waverley
2004	Rev Dr S.H. Rae (April 2004)	First
2005	Mr A. Bayne (from May 2005)	North
2006	Rev Karl Lamb	Lakeside Te Anau
2008	Mr K. Cameron	St. David's
2010	Rev R.J. Gray	First
	Rev R.J. Gray	First

Bibliography

Bell, Hames, Jill Hopkinson, and Trevor Willmott, eds. *Re-Shaping Rural Ministry. A Theological and Practical Handbook.* Norwich, UK: Canterbury, 2009.

Bennett, Bill. 'The pastoral imperative in rural ministry: helping rural people discern God's activity in their midst' (on Rural Ministry in New Zealand) in *Rural Theology: international, ecumenical and interdisciplinary perspectives.* Vol. 5 Part 2/69. 2007. 75-84.

Chisholm, James. *Fifty Years Syne.* Dunedin, NZ: New Zealand Bible Tract and Book Society, 1898.

Collie, John. *The Story of the Otago Free Church Settlement 1848-1948.* Dunedin, NZ: Presbyterian Bookroom, 1948.

Ellis, Hugh. *Ministry, Ministers & Mission in Rural Areas, A Practitioner's Reflections on Rural Ministry.* Unpublished report, 2010.

Hughes, Philip and Audra Kunciunas. eds. *Rural Churches in the Uniting Church in South Australia: Models for Ministry.* Nunawading, Victoria, Australia: Presbytery of South Australia. 2008.

Kennedy, Heather. *Multi-Parish Ministry for Presbyterian Parishes In Southland.* Master of Ministry Research Project, Otago University, 2014

McDonald, Georgina. *The Flame Unquenched. Being the History of the Presbyterian Church in Southland in the Years 1856-1956.* Invercargill, NZ: Presbytery of Southland, 1956.

McKean, John. *The Church in a Special Colony. A History of the Presbyterian Synod of Otago and Southland 1866-1991.* Dunedin, NZ: Synod of Otago and Southland, 1994.

Madill, Crawford. *Part of a Miracle: Profile of a Presbytery – Southland 1956-1990*. Invercargill, NZ: Presbytery of Southland, 1990.

Meade, John M. *People and Ministry, A Future for the Rural Church*. Hedenham, Bungay, Suffolk, UK: Fine. 1994.

Natusch, Sheila. *Brother Wohlers. Te Porora O Ruapuke*. Christchurch, NZ: Pegasus, 1969.

Presbyterian Church of Aotearoa New Zealand. *Book of Order*. Presbyterian Church Archives. Knox College, Arden St., Dunedin, New Zealand.

 https://www.presbyterian.org.nz/sites/default/fils/Book_of_Order_2012_.pdf

Southland Presbytery Minutes. Rural Ministry Conference. *Rural Ministry. Papers presented at the Rural Ministry conference held at Orange on 20-21st August, 1984*. New South Wales: Rural Ministry Unit of the Uniting Church of Australia, NSW Synod, 1984.

Stoner, Rob. *Fresh Directions Developing mission-shaped church and ministry. A Report on Fresh Expressions*. Keswick, South Australia, Australia: Mediacom Education, 2010.

_____ *The Cluster of Congregations with Lay Ministry Teams. The Continuing Story of One Area's Response to the Changing Rural Situation*. Berri, South Australia, Australia: Uniting Church, 2001.

Rural Strategy Team. *God's Own Country. A Practical Resource for Rural Churches,* Edinburgh, UK: Church of Scotland, 2011.

Wells, Stephanie. *Rural Parishes – dying, surviving, thriving: doing ministry beyond the traditional 'one parish-one ordained minister' model*. Study Leave Report, PCANZ, 2011.

 https://www.presbyterian.org.nz/for-ministers/study-leave-reports (Note that this web page is not accessible by the public)

Whitehead, John. 'Countrywide Care', *Journal of Christian Rural Concern*. Editorial. Spring 2011, 2-3.

Index of People